About the authors

Morten Bøås is senior researcher at Fafo Institute for Applied International Studies in Oslo. His recent publications include *Global Institutions and Development: Framing the world?* (with Desmond McNeill, 2004), *New and Critical Security and Regionalism: Beyond the nation state* (with James J. Hentz, 2003), *African Guerrillas: Raging against the machine* (with Kevin Dunn, 2007) and, most recently, *International Development*, Volumes I–IV (with Benedicte Bull, 2010).

Kevin C. Dunn is an associate professor of political science at Hobart and William Smith Colleges in Geneva, NY, USA. His publications include *Imagining the Congo: The international relations of identity* (2003), *Africa's Challenge to International Relations Theory* (with Timothy M. Shaw, 2001), *Identity and Global Politics: Theoretical and empirical elaborations* (with Patricia Goff, 2004) and *African Guerrillas: Raging against the machine* (with Morten Bøås, 2007).

POLITICS OF ORIGIN IN AFRICA

Autochthony, citizenship and conflict

Morten Bøås and Kevin Dunn

Zed Books

LONDON | NEW YORK

Politics of Origin in Africa: Autochthony, citizenship and conflict was first published in 2013 by Zed Books Ltd, 7 Cynthia Street, London N1 9JF, UK and Room 400, 175 Fifth Avenue, New York, NY 10010, USA

www.zedbooks.co.uk

Copyright © Morten Bøås and Kevin Dunn 2013

The rights of Morten Bøås and Kevin Dunn to be identified as the authors of this work have been asserted by them in accordance with the Copyright, Designs and Patents Act, 1988

FSC
www.fsc.org
MIX
Paper from responsible sources
FSC® C013604

Set in Monotype Plantin and FFKievit by Ewan Smith, London
Index: ed.emery@thefreeuniversity.net
Cover design: www.alice-marwick.co.uk
Printed and bound in Great Britain by CPI Group (UK) Ltd, Croydon, CR0 4YY

Distributed in the USA exclusively by Palgrave Macmillan, a division of St Martin's Press, LLC, 175 Fifth Avenue, New York, NY 10010, USA

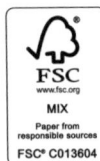

A catalogue record for this book is available from the British Library
Library of Congress Cataloging in Publication Data available

ISBN 978 1 84813 997 8 hb
ISBN 978 1 84813 996 1 pb

CONTENTS

ACKNOWLEDGEMENTS

This manuscript has benefited from conversations, suggestions and assistance from a wide range of colleagues and friends. First and foremost, we would like to thank our editor Ken Barlow and the wonderful people at Zed Books for their work on this project. We would also like to thank Peter Geschiere for his invaluable insights and suggestions. Gratitude also goes out to Karel Arnaut, Ingunn Bjørkhaug, Anna Creadick, Jodi Dean, Iva Deutchman, Barrow and Strummer Dunn, Stephen Ellis, Pierre Englebert, Judith Forshaw, Anne Hatløy, Jim Hentz, Stephen Jackson, Kathleen M. Jennings, Cedric Johnson, René Lemarchand, DeWayne Lucas, David Ost, Paul Passavant, Stacey Philbrick Yadav, Will Reno, Getor Saydee, David Sengel, Tim Shaw, Ian Taylor, Mats Utas, Henrik Vigh, Susie Winters and Vikash Yadav. We would also like to thank our invaluable friends in Côte d'Ivoire, the Democratic Republic of Congo, Kenya and Liberia. Support from the Research Council of Norway for fieldwork in Côte d'Ivoire, DRC and Liberia is also gratefully acknowledged. Finally, we are grateful to one another for the patience and friendship that sustained this project.

ABBREVIATIONS

ADF	Allied Democratic Forces (DRC)
ADIACI	Association pour la Défense des Intérêts des Autochtones de Côte d'Ivoire
AFDL	Alliance des Forces Démocratiques pour la Libération du Congo/Zaïre
ALCOP	All Liberian Coalition Party
ALR	Army for the Liberation of Rwanda
AU	African Union
CNDP	Congrès National pour la Défense du Peuple
CPA	Comprehensive Peace Agreement
DRC	Democratic Republic of Congo
ECK	Electoral Commission of Kenya
ECOWAS	Economic Community of West African States
FAR	Forces Armées Rwandaises
FARDC	Forces Armées de la République Démocratique du Congo
FAZ	Forces Armées Zaïroises
FDLR	Forces Démocratiques pour la Libération du Rwanda
FN	Forces Nouvelles (Côte d'Ivoire)
FPI	Front Populaire Ivoirien
FRCI	Forces Républicaines de Côte d'Ivoire
GSU	General Service Unit (Kenya)
HRW	Human Rights Watch
ICC	International Criminal Court
ICG	International Crisis Group
IDP	internally displaced person
KADU	Kenya African Democratic Union
KANU	Kenya African National Union
KEDOF	Kenya Elections Domestic Observation Forum
KNCHR	Kenya National Commission on Human Rights
KNYA	Kenya National Youth Alliance
LURD	Liberians United for Reconciliation and Democracy
MFA	Mouvement des Forces d'Avenir (Côte d'Ivoire)
MLC	Movement for the Liberation of Congo

MODEL	Movement for Democracy in Liberia
MONUC	United Nations Organisation Mission in the Democratic Republic of Congo
MONUSCO	United Nations Organisation Stabilisation Mission in the Democratic Republic of Congo
NARC	National Alliance of Rainbow Coalition (Kenya)
NPFL	National Patriotic Front of Liberia
NTGL	National Transitional Government of Liberia
ODM	Orange Democratic Movement (Kenya)
ODM-K	Orange Democratic Movement-Kenya
OECD	Organisation for Economic Co-operation and Development
ONUCI	Opération des Nations Unies en Côte d'Ivoire
PARECO	Patriotes Résistants Congolais
PDCI	Parti Démocratique de Côte d'Ivoire
PNU	Party of National Unity (Kenya)
RCD	Rassemblement Congolais pour la Démocratie
RDR	Rassemblement des Républicains (Côte d'Ivoire)
RFDG	Rassemblement des Forces Démocratiques de Guinée
RPF	Rwandan Patriotic Front
RUF	Revolutionary United Front (Sierra Leone)
SLDF	Sabaot Land Defence Force (Kenya)
TWP	True Whig Party (Liberia)
ULIMO	United Liberation Movement of Liberia for Democracy
UN	United Nations
UNHCR	United Nations High Commissioner for Refugees
UNITA	União Nacional para a Independência Total de Angola
UNMIL	United Nations Mission in Liberia

1 | INTRODUCTION: CONFLICT, LAND SCARCITY AND TALES OF ORIGIN

People have always been seeking the attachment of belonging to something. This 'something' can be manifested in land, religion, a flag, an institution or anything else that makes us feel more secure and comfortable. Of course, to include is also to exclude, possibly making others insecure for not belonging. As such, there is nothing new in observing that there are clear connections between claims of belonging and conflict. What is new, however, is the context in which these processes are now taking place, a context of nervousness in which the modern state fails to deliver not only employment and social services to its inhabitants, but also basic notions of security. It is not uncommon to note that many modern states are failing to fulfil their expected material functions, but we suggest that they are also failing at the psychic level. The basic societal 'rules of the game' that the state seems intuitively to underpin are being thrown into question. Such a situation helps foster dreams about a past when things were different; when there was not only food on the table, but also order and opportunity. What this leads to is nostalgia; a melancholy for a seemingly lost past. This is the feeling of having lost something; we may not necessarily be able to articulate the feeling very clearly, but it still seems very dear to us. It is a situation of despair, of loss of direction and purpose. And in the midst of this, one searches both to make sense of that loss and to rectify it.

New narratives can arise to meet those needs, providing an explanation and a solution. One powerful narrative is the claim to autochthony. Autochthony implies that one is entitled to belong because of ancestral rights to land. Simply put, the claim is 'this is ours because we were here first'. There is much wrapped up in these claims, such as assumptions about patriarchal practices, understandings of space, the 'natural' privatisation of land, and, most notably, practices of inclusion and exclusion. At their root, these autochthony tales promise to restore that sense of belonging, often by articulating an implicit political agenda. This is what we mean by 'tales of origin as political cleavage'. They are narratives, discursive constructions, that shape perceptions and inform people's actions by linking identity and space in very specific ways. Our focus in this study is how those tales have become manifested in contemporary African cases, often provoking dramatic expressions of political violence. Of course, these developments are not unique to Africa. Peter Geschiere's (2009) recent work *Perils of Belonging* brilliantly highlights how similar discourses have arisen in both Cameroon and the Netherlands. Conflicts over rights to citizenship, land, employment or state services are not an African phenomenon, but a global development.

The employment of autochthony discourses has become a prominent feature of contemporary politics around the world. Autochthony discourses link identity and space, enabling the speaker to establish a direct claim to territory by asserting that he or she is an original inhabitant, a 'son of the soil'. Autochthony, literally meaning 'emerging from the soil', implies localist forms of belonging, referring to someone with a supposedly indisputable historical link to a particular territory. Its expressions have led to violent struggles in Africa, where assertions of autochthony are used to justify land claims. Indeed, land and autochthony disputes are increasingly the hallmark of political crises in many places on the African continent.

This book, therefore, explores the phenomenon of autochthony in contemporary African politics. The rise of autochthony discourses appears to be a significant aspect of global politics in the current era of globalisation. And while every context is certainly unique, one may well wonder why the employment of autochthony discourses is such a salient feature of so many of today's political conflicts, and why autochthony discourses are so often linked to violence. The rise of exclusionary autochthony discourses in Africa is particularly noteworthy given that, historically, African social formations have generally been characterised by mobility and inclusiveness, with permeable and shifting boundaries. Yet, in recent years, autochthony claims have been part of some of the more striking cases of political violence in Africa. This book combines theoretically oriented chapters that examine the reasons behind the recent rise of autochthony with four chapters that provide in-depth empirical evidence from a handful of case studies from across Africa: Liberia, Kenya, Democratic Republic of Congo (DRC) and Côte d'Ivoire. In all four cases, the population has recently suffered grave forms of political violence in which autochthony claims were central, even if the actual word 'autochthony' is not used in the language of violence in Kenya and Liberia.

Resource scarcity and armed conflict

Over the past thirty years, there have been more than seventy wars fought in Africa. While the end of the Cold War initially heralded a decline in armed struggles on the continent, recent years have witnessed an escalation of conflicts that are increasingly violent and protracted. At the beginning of the twenty-first century, sixteen of Africa's fifty-four countries were affected by armed conflict. On the global level, a common factor among war-prone countries is poverty. The poorest one-sixth of humanity endures roughly four-fifths of the world's civil wars. Many scholars believe that the strong correlation between conflict and poverty needs to be explained. Attention is often paid to the structural causes of deep inequality, the impact of unequal growth, and, increasingly, the unequal distribution of resources.

Recent scholarship has suggested that conflicts in Africa are caused by environmental scarcity and/or economic predation. While there is much to glean from some of this research, we tend to find the analyses wanting, if not misguided. Research, dubbed 'Malthusian' or 'neo-Malthusian' by proponents and critics alike, has explored the relationship between conflict and resource scarcity. Perhaps the most notable author attached to this approach has been Thomas Homer-Dixon, who has proposed that six kinds of environmental scarcity could potentially produce violent conflict: 1) greenhouse effect; 2) stratosphere ozone depletion; 3) degradation and loss of good agricultural land; 4) degradation and removal of forests; 5) depletion and pollution of fresh water supplies; and 6) depletion of fisheries (Homer-Dixon 1994). Homer-Dixon and others have argued that Africa will be particularly susceptible to these forces, given that African states lack 'adaptive capacity' (Homer-Dixon and Blitt 1998: 9). The claim is that economically poor states, which lack both financial and human capital and are ethnically diverse, are less likely to be able to manage the severe environmental challenges that lead to scarcity.

Homer-Dixon's work suggests three hypotheses linking conflict with environmental scarcity. First, it is suggested that decreasing supplies of physically controllable resources would provoke interstate 'simple scarcity' conflicts or 'resource wars'. For example, Michael Klare (2001) has asserted that competition for and control over critical natural resources will be the guiding principles behind the use of military force in the twenty-first century. Second, large population movements caused by environment stress might induce 'group identity' conflicts such as ethnic clashes. Third, severe environmental scarcity would simultaneously increase economic deprivation and disrupt social institutions, namely the state, and cause deprivation conflicts that would be reflected in civil strife and insurgency (Homer-Dixon 1999). For Homer-Dixon and like-minded thinkers, scarcity will be caused by increased demand due to population growth or by increased consumption, and by decreased supply due to erosion, degradation and/ or unequal access and distribution (ibid.: 280). It is Homer-Dixon's contention that scarcity will lead to resource capture by those with the means to do this, and environmental marginalisation of those without means.

It should be noted at the outset that the degree of causality given to environmental factors has varied across Homer-Dixon's published record. Indeed, Homer-Dixon has stepped away from making grand causal claims about the links between resource scarcity and violent conflict. In 1999, he concluded that:

> environmental scarcity is not sufficient, by itself, to cause violence; when it does contribute to violence, research shows, it always interacts with other political, economic, and social factors. Environmental scarcity's causal role can never be separated from these contextual factors, which are often unique to the society in question. (ibid.: 178)

In 2012, the prestigious *Journal of Peace Research* published a special issue on climate change and conflict that challenged a number of 'Malthusian' assumptions, yet causal connections between scarcity and conflict continue to be forwarded by some. A number of writers have been alarmist in their pronouncements and more grandiose in their causal claims. Robert Kaplan (1994), for example, provocatively proclaims that resource scarcity in Africa and elsewhere is directly linked to warfare and increased human misery, with direct implications for the global North.

A number of scholars have expanded on Homer-Dixon's hypotheses regarding 'simple scarcity' conflicts or 'resource wars'. Paul Collier (2000; 2007), for example, has analysed the economic reasons underlying civil wars over the past forty years and concludes that economic greed and control over scarce resources are far stronger explanatory factors than grievance. The works by Collier and others often imply that all African wars are resource wars, fought not over political issues but in order to gain access to profits (see Collier 2000; Berdal and Malone 2000; Klare 2001). Much of this literature argues that changes in the global economy have helped foster the rise of so-called 'new wars' (see Kaldor 1999; Duffield 2001). The argument is that changes in the global economy, particularly the increased interconnectedness of certain markets, have provided new opportunities for African guerrilla movements. Such approaches often mistakenly assume that theft and predation are the *reasons* for the conflict. While we recognise the complex ways in which African guerrilla movements have been exploiting opportunities provided to them by changes in the global political economy, we reject explanations of African armed struggles that focus primarily on the supposed economic agendas of these actors (Bøås and Dunn 2007). Such a myopic focus may help explain how some conflicts are sustained, but it rarely tells us much about why conflicts start in the first place. Likewise, 'Malthusian' arguments that suggest a causal connection between resource scarcity and conflict tend to conflate environmental circumstances with political strategies.

Land and conflict in Africa

Our concern in this book is how the concept of autochthony in the form of tales of origin is deployed in contemporary African conflicts. As we will see, autochthony claims are intimately connected to disputes over land and access to land. While we are concerned with how struggles over a scarce resource such as land are related to armed conflict, we want to be clear that we do not share the assumptions made by the 'neo-Malthusian' and 'resource wars' approaches mentioned above. In general, we think these approaches are fundamentally misguided. For us, it is a political, not environmental or economic, issue. But it behoves us to consider these arguments concerning environmental scarcity in order to get the relationship between land and conflict right.

Approaches that make causal links between scarcity and violent conflict have been strongly challenged by other scholars. Already in the mid-1970s Ester Boserup (1976) exposed some of the problems with the neo-Malthusian approach. As these kinds of theories tend to assume that a given environment has a certain carrying capacity for the human population, they also suggest that, if this point of equilibrium is exceeded, hunger, environmental disaster or conflict will follow until a new equilibrium is reached. The problem with this kind of reasoning, according to Boserup, is that two important factors were ignored. First, these theories focused only on the technology of food production, thus ignoring other types of technological change; and secondly, they ignored the effects of demographic change on both environment and technology. Both technological and institutional innovation could lead societies out of the nightmarish Malthusian scenario, and, as we will see in the case of Liberia and Côte d'Ivoire, local rural populations have responded to the influx of new inhabitants on their territory with various techniques of social engineering. However, these cases also illustrate that social compromises, once made, can also break down and lead to conflict, but there is no immediate or direct link between increased population pressure and conflict. Building on the pioneering work of Boserup and others, there is therefore currently a sizeable weight of scholarly literature that suggests that environmental change rarely causes conflict directly and only occasionally does so indirectly (Kahl 2006; Derman et al. 2007).

Scholars have also pointed out that the reasons for war are usually independent of environmental disruptions such as scarcity, and thus one should be cautious in inferring a simple relationship between increased environmental scarcity and warfare. Lietzmann and Vest (1999: 40), for example, have illustrated that environmental stress need not lead to direct violence. The conflict in Darfur, Sudan has been offered by some neo-Malthusians as an example of a war driven by environmental conditions, namely the drought-related problems the region has suffered for decades. Darfur has been regarded by some as 'the world's first climate change war', as it was dubbed by a 2007 UN Environment Programme report. Yet many scholars have been quick to point out that the origins of conflict are far more complex than this catchy epithet suggests. As Alex de Waal (2007) notes:

> In all cases, significant violent conflict erupted because of political factors, particularly the propensity of the Sudan government to respond to local problems by supporting militia groups as proxies to suppress any signs of resistance. Drought, famine and the social disruptions they brought about made it easier for the government to pursue this strategy.

Looking at the examples of violence in Tanzania, Kenya, Burkina Faso and Zimbabwe, Derman, Odgaard and Sjaastad (2007) found that 'none support the direct link between resource scarcity and violence – in each case a mixture of social inequality, lack of secure land rights, a history of conflicts and the use of land as a political reward' was responsible for conflict taking off. But they also noted that 'tense and volatile situations provide opportunities for manipulation of identities, particularly where land is concerned'.

While we tend to regard neo-Malthusian assumptions and causal claims more than a little problematic, they do raise important considerations about the role of scarce resources, such as land, in the development of armed conflicts. Citing such examples as Burundi, Côte d'Ivoire, Rwanda and Zimbabwe, the World Bank acknowledged in its 2003 report *Land Policies for Growth and Poverty Reduction* that 'deprivation of land rights as a feature of more generalized inequality in access to economic opportunities and low economic growth have caused seemingly minor social or political conflicts to escalate into large-scale conflicts'. Furthermore, in its work on Helping Prevent Violent Conflict, the Organisation for Economic Co-operation and Development (OECD) notes the significance of land-related sources of conflict. It notes that one of the primary causes of political destabilisation – population displacement – is often the result of land dispossession. It also suggests that scarcity of productive land and changes in land tenure systems are contributing factors to violent conflict. Moreover, it notes that any successful post-conflict resolution cannot be effective unless it resolves land-related disputes and ensures that demobilised ex-combatants are able to gain access to land (quoted in Huggins and Clover 2005: 4).

The centrality of land in African societies should not be downplayed. In a continent that remains overwhelmingly agricultural, land continues to lie at the heart of social, economic and political life in most of Africa. There also remains a lack of clarity regarding property rights in contemporary Africa, and land tenure continues to be deeply contested on much of the continent. It should be noted that land remains important not only for farming purposes but also as a speculative asset. As such, it is a highly political, and politicised, resource. As Calestous Juma (1996) observed:

The way land use is governed is not simply an economic question, but also a critical aspect of the management of political affairs. It may be argued that the governance of land use is the most important political issue in most African countries.

For us, land and land tenure are important political issues in Africa. But the extent to which they are related to armed conflict depends on the extent to which they are politicised. Attempts to connect land and identity through autochthony discourses are, first and foremost, *political* strategies, and we treat them as such.

Outline of the book

It is important to remember that land insecurity does not, in itself, lead necessarily to armed conflict. Not all countries suffer land scarcity or inequality in access to land. As the cases in this volume illustrate, political entrepreneurs often are able to manipulate land issues to further personal gains. In Africa, and elsewhere, access to land is often interwoven with ethnic dimensions, as land use patterns and customary land tenure systems have historically had an ethnic basis; this is something that colonialism institutionalised into the modern state in many parts of Africa. This has meant that important issues around citizenship and migration – specifically those relating to claims of autochthony – come into play and can gain such powerful salience.

Thus, in Africa, land rights issues are increasingly becoming vulnerable to the politics of identity and belonging (Hagberg 2004). Where land is perceived as scarce, one important advantage may be the ability to stake your claim to land from the position of being autochthonous, or a 'son of the soil', whereas your counterpart is presented as a 'newcomer', an 'immigrant' or a 'stranger'. In such situations, being recognised as a true citizen of the political unit in question (i.e. the country, region, city or village) is of primary importance: although 'citizenship does not entitle you to resources, it entitles you to enter the struggle for resources' (Mamdani 2002: 505). As the four case studies presented in this book illustrate, such conflicts take place within a delimited territory where two or more groups have 'shared' the land for a period of time. Due to a combination of political and economic factors, the compromise upon which their cohabitation was built has become unmanageable. New modes of deciding who has a right to land must therefore be established. In some cases, the conflict can be dealt with by referring to a contract. However, in the cases described in this book, this is rarely possible. There are multiple reasons for this, including unclear 'rules of the game' or because the state has undermined the legitimacy of those rules. In such situations, the exclusion of others based on a claim that they are not autochthonous may seem an effective strategy. However, it may also be the case that more than one group claims the status of autochthony, and thereby the moral right to land. Autochthony discourses therefore often have the character of a Pandora's box: they have no limits or end – in an area infested with autochthony debates, a person can go to bed as autochthonous and wake up the next morning and discover that his status has changed. It is a debate that by its very nature is slippery and fluid. One of our conclusions is that the employment of autochthony and the anxiety it produces leads political agents to act in an ad hoc, short-sighted and purely tactical manner, often at odds with long-term strategic interests.

Our theoretical assumptions about autochthony and its place in contemporary African politics are developed in greater detail in Chapter 2. We begin with the view that the contemporary employment of autochthony discourses in Africa needs to be placed within a historical context that recognises both the impact of pre-colonial ways of being and colonial practices, and the ontological uncertainty of the post-colonial condition. On the one hand, political conflicts over citizenship and 'who belongs' are not a new phenomenon on the African continent. Their origins can be found in both pre-colonial practices and ideas about the politics of place embedded in the colonial project. After independence, citizenship laws increased in importance, as new African states had to permanently define who lived legitimately within the borders of their territories and who did not. This creation of 'foreigners' brought about by impending independence led to riots in many places as early as the 1950s and 1960s (see Crook 1997). Thus, to a certain degree, conflicting claims concerning citizenship and land rights are not new but are an enduring part of African history that is better seen along the lines of *la longue durée*. On the other hand, it must be recognised that for autochthony discourses to be politically effective, they must resonate with a large enough segment of the population of the political territory in question. So, while it is true that autochthony is neither new nor exclusively an African phenomenon, it is clear that it is gaining in its political salience in many African cases. We contend that the production and employment of autochthony discourses are an attractive response (one of several possible) to the ontological uncertainty of the current post-colonial condition.

The following chapter will explore the multiple contributing factors to this uncertainty, each of which is shaped by the unique context of the specific case. In general, autochthony discourses appear to provide a sense of primal security and certainty, yet they are inherently unstable and slippery. This plasticity is one of the reasons for autochthony's attractiveness, but it is also one of the factors in its close relationship with violence. We maintain that autochthony functions as a trope, without any substance of its own, within the process of constituting political identities, a process that revolves around questions of citizenship and the concept of the citizen as the bearer of rights. Given its malleability, in reality autochthony increases political anxiety, particularly in the lived experiences of Africans. One of our core contentions is that autochthony discourses must be understood as a political phenomenon, part of the desire for order inherent in contemporary state-making practices. Thus, an investigation of autochthony necessitates a critical examination of contemporary African political practices.

Each of the book's middle four chapters will explore a case study: Liberia (Chapter 3), Kenya (Chapter 4), Democratic Republic of Congo (Chapter 5) and Côte d'Ivoire (Chapter 6). These chapters are built upon in-depth fieldwork as well as secondary literature. The fieldwork material that was collected through a combination of ethnographic interviews and a survey of about 1,500 households enables the production of more systematic information and analysis of how the politics of autochthony are played out within the context of disputes over land rights. The book's contribution to debates on contemporary African politics and conflicts is centred on its cross-country comparisons based on in-depth fieldwork. While the four cases are quite disparate and unique, the politics in each case are organised around slippery scales of autochthony. Once we recognise that autochthony is used in framing certain political debates, we should also become aware of striking similarities – commonalities best described as 'tales of origin as political cleavage'.

The book's concluding chapter connects the four cases studies to the politics of autochthony elsewhere in Africa and the world, establishing conclusions and lessons for research and policy. As the book will repeatedly illustrate, the politics of autochthony are by definition slippery, as this discourse both underwrites and trumps kin, ethnicity and other elements of identity. They are at work within, as well as between, ethnic groups. But even if the use of autochthony discourses differs, they always relate to stories concerning first-comer/latecomer status. At the heart of the argument are citizenship issues and the right to land, but in some cases, such as in DRC and the Côte d'Ivoire, also the right to vote and to stand for election. However, the most crucial factor is the right to land: belonging to the land is in essence what guarantees the rights of present as well as future generations. If there is a perception that this right is being threatened, it must be protected at all costs, and in societies facing ontological uncertainty from multiple angles – from the economic upheaval relating to globalisation to crises in the neopatrimonial state – security can be found in tales of origin. Storytelling about a collective 'we' can entail anything from the nuclear family to the lineage, the community, the ethnic group or several ethnic groups, but almost exclusively this storytelling necessitates a perceived stranger: an other, an intruder, an enemy, somebody threatening certain rights that are seen as the heritage belonging to the 'sons of the soil'. Viewed in this manner, external forces – be they warlords, elites or international actors – are less important. What we are left with is the intertwining of a series of local conflicts into a lager pattern; a war zone that evolves and develops as local communities – dazzled and confused by the events unfolding in their midst – try to protect what they believe belongs to them (see Bøås 2009a). In this regard, this book also offers an alternative explanation of conflict in Africa that is currently missing in the mainstream literature.

- , AUTOCHTHONY, MELANCHOLY AND UNCERTAINTY IN CONTEMPORARY AFRICAN POLITICS

Autochthony is a strategy, not a fact. Proving one is indigenous is an impossible task, yet there is much to be gained by making such an assertion. The employment of claims of autochthony is partly an attempt to reify essentialist claims about identity, to obscure the reality that identification is a dynamic process. After all, identification becomes rigid or flexible depending on the circumstances. To make a claim of autochthony is to treat identity as a concrete reality and, more importantly, to draw a line between those who belong and those who do not. The rise of exclusionary autochthony discourses in Africa is particularly noteworthy given that historically African social formations have generally been characterised by mobility and inclusiveness, with permeable and shifting boundaries. One characteristic of pre-colonial Africa was the porousness of identity boundaries and a general openness to others. As historian John Lonsdale (2008a: 311) has noted: 'African inter-regional relations have hitherto been marked by efforts to assimilate as much as to exclude useful strangers, to accept new citizens as well as to conscript fresh slaves.' Yet today we find not only a rise in autochthony claims across Africa, but also their employment to legitimise political violence. How does one explain this development?

The melancholy of autochthony

What do people do when they believe that they have lost, or are in the process of losing, something dear? A number of options are available, ranging from taking immediate action – manifest or latent as well as violent or peaceful – to seeking refuge in the spiritual realm. Regardless of the response, one needs to make sense of the loss; to have an explanation of why the loss has occurred and, more often than not, who is to blame. This involves a process of narrating memory, of constructing tales of what is remembered and, not least, of what one can afford to remember.

The full luxury of memory is something few of us can afford or even dare to confront, but the more difficult, uncertain and violent a life-world is, the more important certain trajectories of memory become. These are first and foremost the memories understood as helpful: the kind of politics of memory that makes it possible to construct an understanding of one's trying circumstance. These are the narratives that can offer comfort in the face of uncertainty because they carry with them the idea that it does not have to be like this; that this is not how it is supposed to be, and that another trajectory of life once existed and can be brought back – perhaps only if those who have caused this situation can be expelled or brought under control.

What this kind of narrative and remembering often leads to is a nostalgia for a lost past. This can create a collective sense of melancholy, where people and groups feel that they have been deprived of something very dear to them, without necessarily being able to articulate very clearly what this actually was. Nonetheless, at the same time it provides with 'dead certainty' someone who is responsible for their predicament, who is to blame for this state of despair. When and if this happens, the lack of direction that results from despair can vanish and be replaced by a potentially violent certainty. This is quite similar to what Freud (1913) talked about in his book *Totem and Taboo*, where he conjures up the nervous unease of that particular period, and how political, religious, scientific and artistic agitation drummed up these types of sentiments, drawing upon them but also facilitating and strengthening them. Melancholy in this sense can only be diagnosed, not cured, and therefore Freud saw it as one of the most serious of a range of possible human psychological conditions.

We are not arguing that a path-dependent version of this argument should be applied to our case studies. For example, Freud considered melancholy incurable because of the patient's unwillingness to face the real source of his or her melancholy, which implies a degree of paralysis.[1] Yet, as the chapters that follow so tragically illustrate, autochthony can be anything but paralysing as it has the potential to inspire people to feverish action and unfettered violence. Yet there are aspects of melancholy – from its nervous unease and poetic sadness to the inability to face its real sources of loss and the resentment that loss inspires (see McGovern 2011: 67–102) – that we believe we meet when we enter the field of eastern DRC, the western regions of Côte d'Ivoire, the borderland that straddles Liberia, Sierra Leone and Guinea, and the Rift Valley settler schemes and slums of urban Kenya, and we treat melancholy as a frame that can help us decipher something important about the modern condition as it manifests itself in troubled states on the African continent.

This is the melancholy of the social angst of uncertainty created by modern life in Africa and beyond. However, this is also a condition that does not entail the kind of closure that is brought about by lesser manifestations of uncertainty. Rather, it is the opposite; it fuels its own spiralling condition. That is, this type of modern melancholy can lead to an intense sadness as the reaction of those scapegoated all too predictably seek their own melancholic tunes. They revisit their own stories of lineage, people, place and exceptionalism, and therein find the means to construct their own violent melancholies. Mahmood Mamdani (2001) captured this scenario when he entitled his study of the 1994 Rwandan genocide *When Victims Become Killers*. The perpetrators justify their violence through memories of their own victimhood, and in the process produce more victims and potential future killers. An obscure rebellion in Côte d'Ivoire in 1970 – of which only Jean-Pierre Dozon (1985) and Mike McGovern (2011) have seen the importance – further illustrates this point. In Gagnoa, a man named Nragbé Kragbé led a revolt against the country's founding father Houphouët-Boigny. The revolt was short-lived and accomplished little more than the symbolic announcement of an 'Eburnien Republic' and the lowering of the Ivorian flag from some government buildings in Gagnoa. Quite predictably, it ended with a small massacre, as the rebels did not have any chance against the Ivorian state. Symbolically, however, this event carried with it much greater ramifications as the discourse it created cemented Bété sentiments of exclusion and marginalisation from the state and from the non-autochthonous immigrants perceived as taking over the rich forest land of the Bété with the blessing of the state. As such, the narrative it helped create was one that combined marginalisation and exclusion with resistance, thereby constructing a powerful story about the exceptionalism of people and place that Laurent Gbagbo would make good use of decades later (ibid.: 83).

What this example underscores is why claims to autochthony have been such an integral part of some of the more striking cases of political violence in Africa. From Rwanda, DRC, Kenya and Côte d'Ivoire, 'sons of the soil' have been killing people they portrayed as 'invading aliens' seeking to grab power and land. As noted earlier, Mamdani

(2002) has made a strong argument that autochthony was also a pronounced aspect of the 1994 Rwandan genocide, where extremists opposed the government's redefinition of Rwandan political identities and refused to regard Tutsi as anything but a non-indigenous race. When members of the Tutsi diaspora initiated their armed repatriation from neighbouring Uganda, the *genocidaires* responded as autochthons, killing people they perceived as alien settlers. As the next four chapters illustrate, the concept of autochthony also informs the continuing conflict in eastern DRC, Côte d'Ivoire, Liberia and Kenya.

But what explains the recent rise of violent autochthony claims in a continent historically characterised by mobility and inclusiveness? While every answer needs to be contingent on local realities and unique historical developments, we argue that the recent employment of autochthony discourses is an attractive response – one of several possible – to the ontological uncertainty and mode of melancholy that have come to characterise the modern post-colonial condition in much of Africa. We suggest that there are multiple contributing factors to this melancholy of uncertainty, each of which is shaped by the unique context of each case. In response, autochthony discourses appear to provide a sense of primal security and certainty, yet they are inherently unstable and slippery. The very plasticity of autochthony is one of the reasons for its attractiveness, but also one of the factors underlying its close relationship with violence. As Arjun Appadurai (1999: 322) has argued:

> Uncertainty about identification and violence can lead to actions, reactions, complicities, and anticipations that multiply the pre-existing uncertainty about labels. Together, these forms of uncertainty call for the worst kind of certainty: dead certainty.

In the next section of this chapter, we explore several reasons why the current modern post-colonial condition is characterised by increasing degrees of ontological uncertainty. One of our core contentions is that autochthony discourses are part of the desire for order inherent in contemporary state-making practices, practices that invariably rely on multiple manifestations of violence. Throughout this chapter, we want to maintain a focus on how the autochthony trope is part of the production, reproduction and performance of political identities, which are an inherent part of modern African politics. And we must not forget that autochthony is not a historical fact.

Autochthony and ontological uncertainty

In certain contexts, employing autochthony discourses is an attractive response to the ontological uncertainty of the post-colonial condition. Of course, it is one of several possible responses, and there is a startling variety of autochthony discourses at work across the African continent, as well as in non-African contexts. Indeed, both the seeming ubiquity and the diversity of the autochthony trope make it an interesting phenomenon. It is our contention that there has been a convergence of factors – on multiple levels – that have led to the rise of melancholic uncertainty and thus autochthony claims across much of Africa. In this section we will briefly discuss some of the primary factors that have contributed to today's ontological uncertainty, and subsequently to the sense of loss and melancholy.

Globalisation It has become almost *de rigueur* to begin any conversation on contemporary politics with a reference to the process of 'globalisation', however ill defined the concept. One way of thinking about the term is in reference to the recent set of transitions in the global political economy whereby transnational, flexible and irregular forms of capitalist organisation have become increasingly more pronounced, as labour, finance, technology and technological capital are assembled in ways that treat national boundaries as mere constraints or fictions (ibid.: 307). For some scholars, the processes of globalisation have increased localism and are tied to a rise in violence, inspiring what Mary Kaldor has labelled 'new wars' (1999; see also Clark 1997).

But before we turn to a discussion of recent economic restructuring and its impact on African societies, we want to offer a longer view of history, one that argues that the practice of colonialism has been integral to the process of 'globalisation'. Today's international political and economic systems are, after all, the products of European colonisation and conquest that culminated during the nineteenth and twentieth centuries. As we will note in each of the four cases studied in this volume, the process of colonialism has contributed intimately (and uniquely) to the development of autochthony in modern African politics. In many cases, narratives of historical grievances that contribute to the melancholic uncertainty have their roots in colonial disruptions and administrative injustices. But, for our purposes here, we want to flag just three important and relevant aspects of colonialism that can generally be recognised across the continent. The first is the reification (if not outright invention in some cases) of communal identification within African societies. Colonialism may not have invented ethnicity, but colonial administrative practices certainly made what were flexible forms of identity more rigid and politically relevant. The second is the changes colonialism wrought in terms of how nature was conceptualised. In general, nature was understood in pre-colonial Africa as an open space, usually differentiated into known and named water and land resources and sacred sites. With the advent of colonialism, nature became demarcated as 'territory', divided by international, regional and ethnic borders. Space became 'tamed', fixed and stabilised; an 'immobile closed system' (Massey 2005: 55; see also Watson 2010). The first two developments became related, as African colonial states administered through practices that connected reified ethnic categories to closed territorial systems. That is, under colonialism, identity and land became intertwined in significant ways. This situation is linked to the third aspect: the legal privatisation of land, increasingly conceptualised as a material resource. Often these legal practices (such as the issuing of land titles) were introduced to morally legitimise the accumulation of fertile farmland by Europeans (or, in the case of Liberia, Americo-Liberians), often achieved through coercion and the violent displacement of existing inhabitants. The colonial (and then post-colonial) state underpinned the legal demarcation of land, but, as we will note in the various case studies, it often did so in quite uneven and arbitrary ways, creating a situation that increased not only the importance of land ownership but also the uncertainty of land claims. All three of these elements have contributed, in varying ways, to the melancholic uncertainty of the modern African condition.

In more recent years, we can note how the processes of global economic restructuring have also contributed to this modern condition of uncertainty and insecurity. With regards to Africa, two linked processes are of primary significance: transnationalism and deterritorialisation, and the atomised nature of global capitalism's interaction with Africa's 'new' economy. With the economic liberalisation and decentralisation that have characterised contemporary globalisation, the open-ended global flows of modern capitalism have further helped foster trends of transnationalism in Africa, where borders and boundaries function more as opportunities and conduits rather than as obstacles. The flow of peoples across Africa's internal borders has long been a characteristic of life on the continent, with conflicting economic, political and social implications. The flow of migrants and refugees puts further pressure on land claims and overtaxed economic and ecological systems of survival. This has had a significant effect on subject formation, as the process of transnationalism 'accentuates the conflict between a cosmopolitan and a nativist vision of identity and of African culture' (Mbembe 2001: 1). Of course, this is not a uniquely African phenomenon. As Birgit Meyer and Peter Geschiere (1999: 2) observe:

> There is much empirical evidence that people's awareness of being involved in open-ended global flows seems to trigger a search for fixed orientation points and action frames, as well as determined efforts to affirm old and construct new boundaries.

In response to flux and flow are the concomitant impulses to control and fix. Therefore, the open flows of globalisation have triggered the construction of new boundaries, the reaffirmation of old ones, and the closure of identities.

What is uniquely African is the continent's relationship with the atomistic nature of global capital. Unlike in other parts of the globe, where transnationalisation has been the result of direct foreign investment or the rapid spread of new informational technologies, globalisation's primary impact on the continent has been the emergence of new extractive structures, new extractive regimes – anywhere from Abidjan to Kinshasa, from Monrovia to Nairobi – and mechanisms that have created fragmented spaces that function as a source of both resources and power, enabling local elites and regimes to sell cheaply and benefit handsomely. As Mbembe (2001: 5) argues:

> An atomized capitalism has developed over the debris of a rent economy formerly dominated on one side by state companies controlled by the factions in power, and on the other side by monopolies for the most part dating from the colonial era and operating in captive markets... It has been replaced by a diffracted economy, without any obvious natural core, which is composed of several nodes entangled with one another and which maintain changing and extremely complex relationships with the local environment and with regional and international networks. What emerges is an increasingly polymorphic economic geography in

which territoriality is differentiated and parcelized among multiple institutional and regulatory forms that are not clustered around a single predominant centre of gravity. From this extreme fragmentation has emerged, often within the same country, a multiplicity of economic territorialities, occasionally nested in each other and often separate.

As the examples of Liberia, Kenya, DRC and Côte d'Ivoire will illustrate, access to land is an integral part of these processes, as well as an outcome of them, and has consequently also been a central feature of recent conflicts. Currently, in many African contexts, one finds shifting discourses and practices around land and space, often shaped by the processes of globalisation. Transnationalism and the increased spatial fragmentation caused by the forces of atomistic capitalism have simultaneously introduced new representations of space and created greater demand for land. In the resulting situation, new livelihoods have emerged that are no longer bound within the self-enclosed territorial definitions of the sovereign state. New representations of long distance and migration have emerged, with the concomitant practices of immigration and displacement. One result of globalisation's 'open horizons' for many Africans has been the fragmentation of space, increased boundary construction, and conflicting discourses around identity and belonging. These new developments need to be seen against the longer historical background of capitalism in Africa, where the imposition and maintenance of capitalist labour relations required not only the freeing of labour but also its containment and compartmentalisation (Geschiere and Nyamnjoh 2000). As the later chapters will illustrate, local subject formation is shaped by a number of forces – from commercial and religious networks to secret societies, vigilante groups and militias – that often employ autochthony tropes in the construction of political identities in order to obscure other cleavages and political hierarchies and to achieve a degree of certainty and security. The employment of autochthony discourses is thus both a response to and an integral part of the globalisation process in Africa.

The modern African state Some scholars have argued that the exclusionary practices of autochthony emerge in the vacuum created by the collapse of the African state, an assertion that we will explore within all four case studies. However, we want to make the argument at the tset that ontological uncertainty is related to the ongoing practices of state-making across the globe. There is an inherent tension within the process of state-making, with the state both creating ontological uncertainty and offering itself as the solution to that uncertainty. Perhaps the best articulation of this process and the inherent conflict within the state-making process can be found in Roxanne Doty's examination of desire and governmentality in the immigration practices of contemporary western democracies. Like Doty, we begin with the assumption that there is no such thing as 'the state', only discourses, practices and rituals that call it into being (Dunn 2009). As Doty (2003: 12) argues:

> There is no such thing as 'the state', only a powerful desire for 'the state' that pervades the social realm. Of course, there are governmental bureaucracies and institutions, and human subjects engaging in practices. But these, neither individually nor collectively, are 'the state'. 'The state' is nothing but a desire that is manifested in *practices of statecraft*, practices that can originate in government bureaucracies and institutions, churches, schools, corporations, theatres, novels, art museums, our backyards, our front yards, our kitchens, and living rooms and bedrooms. Practices of statecraft can come from anywhere and from anyone.

In order to produce the appearance of a solid entity, practices of statecraft, or what can be referred to as state-making processes, revolve around the construction and employment of sovereignty discourses in an attempt to control borders and produce the illusion of a clearly defined interior separated from an exterior (Dunn 2010). For Doty (2003: 74–5), 'the state' is primarily 'a desire for order, a desire to overcome ambiguity and uncertainty'. The process of state-making is one that involves a double move: producing ontological uncertainty (about identity, space, time and meaning) and positing the sovereign state as the solution to that uncertainty. Thus, state-making processes rely on the production of ontological crises, producing anxiety about order and welfare, uncertainty about territory and space, insecurity about identity and who belongs. For Doty, at the heart of this process is desire, which is articulated so forcefully in immigration debates:

> This non-place that immigration so insistently points us towards is precisely where desire lurks; within anxieties about order, divisions

between the inside and the outside, insecurities over who belongs
and who does not. This is where desire does its productive work.
This is where we must look for 'the state'. (ibid.: 6)

Uncertainty about political identities is thus an inherent part of
the state-making project. Žižek (1989) refers to this as 'national para-
noia', where the nation is intrinsically nervous about its completeness
and authenticity. In his discussion of autochthony in DRC, Stephen
Jackson (2006: 116) connects these discourses with the contingency
of the Congolese nation. Indeed, all national projects are profoundly
contingent.

In the modern era, the task of order inherent in the state-making
process has become increasingly volatile. As Bauman (1991) suggests,
'order as a task' is arguably the least possible among the impossible
tasks that modernity sets for itself, but also the least disposable among
the indispensable. Within this process, the desire for governmentality
is produced and justified. Of course, governmentality is never stable,
always contested, always being produced and reproduced. The utilisation of autochthony tropes within these processes becomes a very
attractive option, as we discuss later in this chapter.

These processes are not unique to Africa. However, two aspects
of the African state that need to be examined are the recent ex-
periments with political liberalisation and the continuing centrality
of neopatrimonialism. Whether spawned by grassroots pressure or
due to externally imposed conditionalities, political liberalisation has
often been a feature of the process of globalisation in Africa. The
opening up of political space has frequently had the unforeseen effect
of increasing ontological uncertainty as questions of political identity
are pushed to the forefront. Debates concerning citizenship and the
nation have often turned quite violent, as in Rwanda, DRC, Liberia,
Côte d'Ivoire and elsewhere. Ironically and tragically, democratisation has often stimulated an obsession with autochthony and ethnic
citizenship. As Geschiere and Nyamnjoh (2000: 423) note:

Political liberalisation leads, somewhat paradoxically, to an intensi-
fication of the politics of belonging: fierce debates on who belongs
where, violent exclusion of 'strangers' (even if this refers to people
with the same nationality who have lived for generations in the
area), and a general affirmation of roots and origins as the basic
criteria of citizenship and belonging.

In many cases, political liberalisation has helped foster a non-liberal move towards closure and exclusion. For example, the 1991 National Conference in the DRC not only chose to introduce highly stringent citizenship laws but also denied the Banyarwanda delegation admission to the conference.

Political liberalisation can potentially reopen debates over citizenship and belonging, throwing political identities into flux. With democratisation, three key questions emerge: 'Who can vote?', 'Where can they vote?' and 'Who can stand as a candidate?' – questions not often asked under authoritarian rule as there was simply little reason to ask them. This was certainly the case in Côte d'Ivoire when the founding father Houphouët-Boigny died. This uncertainty, this nervousness, and therefore also a sense of melancholy that could turn into rage against the 'other' and that unbalanced social life, did not materialise out of the blue. It had been there for a long time in Ivorian society, but it was mainly expressed only in silence. It was only when the 'old man' had died that these discourses not only entered the public domain but came to dominate it completely. So why was this the case? It was due to this very nervousness – everybody was afraid, nervous and uncertain about what would come next, and answers could be found in the melancholic narratives of marginalisation and exclusion, belonging, land and exceptionalism of both people and place. These answers suited certain elites eager to assume power now that the 'father' had gone, but they also made sense to different audiences as they promised not only certainty but an easily grasped explanation of why life had turned out as it had. Autochthony discourses, therefore, can be deeply embedded in all three questions, as issues of citizenship and belonging gain increased relevance in the formation of political identities.

In numerous African cases, the employment of autochthony tropes becomes quite pronounced as countries move towards political liberalisation. In cases such as Rwanda, DRC and Côte d'Ivoire, a democratic majority has used the democratic process to disenfranchise a minority. Each of these cases illustrates how autochthony discourses are employed within the process of political liberalisation to redefine citizenship on narrow and exclusionary terms, thus codifying political identities and allegiances, and turning belonging to a certain group of people into individual political alignments. In other cases, such as Kenya, where no single ethnic group dominates the electorate, political liberalisation and the reintroduction of multiparty politics have encouraged politicians to activate ethnic discourses that, in some cases, hinge on melancholic autochthony claims. That is, electoral politics are presented as opportunities to right historic 'wrongs' committed by 'aliens' and 'strangers'. We will examine the reasons why politicians in each of the four case studies have opted to politicise ethnicity and employ autochthony as a political strategy, but in almost every case they relate to crises developing in the post-colonial neopatrimonial state.

In recent years, the African state has entered an era of crisis caused by multiple forces, such as the shrinking of central government under structural adjustment programmes and the increased marginalisation of Africa in the world economy. As a result, the Westphalian sovereign state model, inherited from colonialism and modified according to the needs of African ruling elites, is in severe crisis across the continent, although the manifestations of that crisis are varied and geographically uneven. Some have suggested that the rise of autochthony discourses relates to the collapse of the African state in the face of globalisation processes. Such a view is founded on mistaken assumptions about the African state, its performativity and its role in globalisation processes. We suggest that what are really in 'crisis' are the neopatrimonial networks and practices traditionally underpinning the African state.

Neopatrimonialism should be considered as a mixed type of rule that combines various degrees of differentiation and lack of separation between public and private spheres, creating a context where bureaucratic rationality and patrimonial norms coexist (Médard 1991). While this is a general characteristic of most contemporary states, the patrimonial aspects have been pronounced in many African cases (Braathen, Bøås and Sæther 2000). In the immediate post-colonial era, neopatrimonial systems of rule proved to be remarkably stable in many countries, even producing 'strong' regimes in 'weak' states (Zaire, Kenya, Sierra Leone, Malawi, Côte d'Ivoire, to name but a few). In some cases, such as Côte d'Ivoire, the logic of neopatrimonialism strengthened the relevance of the autochthony trope (Marshall-Fratani 2006: 20). In other cases, access to neopatrimonial patron–client relationships was less strongly tied to autochthonous notions of belonging. In DRC, Mobutu's neopatrimonial system of rule sometimes relied on the subversion of autochthony tropes as he rewarded personal loyalty over all else. At other times, such as towards the end of his reign, he exploited autochthony tropes and xenophobia quite effectively (Dunn 2003).

The success of African neopatrimonial networks relies on the ability of political elites to fulfil the expected vertical redistribution of resources through the patron–client relationship. What has happened recently in many African neopatrimonial states is a failure to deliver on the promises of the patronage system. The capacity of ruling elites to maintain the systems of reciprocity on which the patron–client relationship relies has been undermined. As a result, there has emerged both a crisis of legitimacy for the ruling elites and the perceived bankruptcy of the established state system. As the crisis of neopatrimonialism unfolds, political identities that were based on these seemingly stable systems of patronage are increasingly in flux. Thus, the ontological certainty provided by neopatrimonialism has begun to unravel, and one option has been an increased utilisation of autochthony discourses to exclude competitors in the struggle for the political and economic resources associated with state power.

Regional big men, private militias and marginalised youths It is one of our core observations that the rise of autochthony within African conflicts is due to its employment by regional big men. This is significant because we are arguing that autochthony's rise is not primarily due to a grassroots development, but rather to a top-down employment of nativist claims by regional leaders as part of explicit political strategies. It should be noted at the outset that modern African politics have become characterised by the growing importance of regional big men (Utas 2012). This is in large part related to the existence of neopatrimonial systems, in which regional big men function as central nodes within the networks of vertical redistribution. In cases where the African state has engaged in political liberalisation, the importance of regional big men has grown as they have become vital in the political mobilisation of constituencies (or, as we shall see, in the suppression of oppositional electoral groups) for electoral gain. In cases where formal state structures recede or collapse, such as in Liberia and DRC, regional big men become important alternative sites of authority and governance.

The reasons why regional big men have employed autochthony as a political strategy vary across the cases studied. Suffice it to say, there is a growing belief in the political salience of such strategies. This is due to the fact that, in the cases we examine, they are met with popular approval; that is to say, even if autochthony is being deployed as a top-down political strategy, it enjoys a fair degree of popular traction. The reasons for this relate to autochthony's promise of providing answers and solution for the melancholic uncertainty of the modern African condition. But it is imperative not to equate the general popularity of autochthony claims in some areas with assumptions about mass participation in its violent articulation. While autochthony might be seen by many as legitimising violence, more often than not most political violence is committed by a limited number of groups. As our case studies illustrate, these groups tend to be made up of marginalised young men who often operate with the support, patronage and funding of regional big men.

In many ways, the rise of private militias reflects the decentral-isation of violence that has come to characterise much of modern African politics. Robert Bates (2008) has argued that this situation has arisen as societies have militarised against a failing state executive. As the African state is privatised and gutted from the inside, internal elements (usually led by regional big men) militarise for their own political enrichment and survival, undercutting the state's claim to the legitimate monopoly of violence. While there is a degree of truth in Bates' observations, it overstates the argument to a significant extent. As our cases will illustrate, African societies have also militarised *through* the executive. As the examples of Kenya and Côte d'Ivoire so graphically show, existing gangs of marginalised youths originally emerged for economic reasons but were co-opted by the state ex-ecutive. They are deployed violently against rival communities for political purposes, and then dropped from patronage. These militias tend not to disappear completely but rather fade back into society, fall under the patronage of opposition leaders, or become general enemies of the state (see Branch and Cheeseman 2008). The result is the militarisation of society by the state, not in the absence of it. It is not difficult to observe how this development has contributed to the insecurity and uncertainty of modern African politics.

The perpetrators of most autochthonous violence in Africa have been young men, usually operating within private militias or armed gangs. They tend to be the unfortunate by-product of a number of generational disruptions and collapsing social networks that relate to the crises of neopatrimonial systems of power within modern African politics. As established patron–client relationships unravel, there are growing groups of youths who are increasingly marginalised – economically, politically and socially. For many of these youths, life is characterised by acute ontological uncertainty and vulnerability. For many, joining armed groups and militias is both a means of survival and a mode of production and accumulation (Bøås and Dunn 2007; Bøås and Hatløy 2008). As Ruth Marshall-Fratani (2006: 31) notes in the case of Côte d'Ivoire:

> With the encouragement of local authorities and regional dignitaries with important positions in Abidjan, groups of 'young village patriots' have created a climate of terror in which strangers (northerners, Burkinabé, but also Baoulé) are chased off their land, which subsequently is seized 'legally' by local big men. In this process of expropriation, the youth use violence, but they also pose as defenders of a 'tradition' which they accuse their elders of having abandoned. Thus they reaffirm not only their autochthonous rights to land but also their growing ascendancy vis-à-vis the older generations.

Indeed, the role of the youth in stressing questions of national belonging, employing autochthony discourses and resorting to violence should not be underestimated. Youth is already a liminal category *par excellence*, and youths are also frequently the principal victims of socio-economic crises. In the Côte d'Ivoire and elsewhere, the armed conflict provides youths with an opportunity for empowerment and the renegotiation of their status. Thus, it should not be surprising that youth are often deeply involved in employing autochthony tropes and violence. As we discuss below, the trope (and its violent underpinnings) is an attractive response for socially marginalised groups who are dealing with ontological uncertainty.

The inherent paradox of autochthony discourses

Certainly, there is a long tradition of autochthony discourse in the history of mankind. It is neither new nor exclusively African. Historically, political entrepreneurs have employed the trope of autochthony for a wide array of reasons. But for the trope to work, it must resonate with a large enough sector of the population. We are concerned with why the autochthony trope is gaining traction in

Africa. Our core argument is that, in certain contexts, it is proving to be an attractive response to the ontological uncertainty of modern post-colonial African life because it provides the illusion of primal certainty and security.

As we discussed above, the growing multiplicity and contingency of identities available to individuals in the contemporary world can produce a daunting sense of uncertainty about people, places, events and even cosmologies. In the face of concerns such as globalisation's 'open horizons', the arbitrariness of the modern neopatrimonial state and the decentralisation of violence in daily life, the desire for closure and the construction of boundaries can be quite strong. Indeed, the practice of exclusion may provide a sense of belonging for those seemingly adrift. Peter Geschiere (2009) has referred to this desire as 'a global conjecture of belonging', where the apparently unrelated trends of political and economic liberalisation, decentralisation, ecological anxieties and fears over the loss of culture seem to converge in deepening concerns about belonging (see also Li 2000). As Geschiere and Nyamnjoh (2000: 424) observe:

> Autochthony seems to go together very well with globalisation.
> It creates a feeling of belonging, yet goes beyond ethnicity's
> specificity. Precisely because of its lack of substance it appears to
> be a tempting and therefore all the more dangerous reaction to
> seemingly open-ended global flows.

Part of the appeal of the autochthony trope is that it seems to be so clearly self-evident to those who employ it. In comparison with ethnicity, which conjures up some sort of core meaning in an essentialised ethnic identity, autochthony relies on nothing but the claim to have been in a certain space first. Geschiere and Jackson (2006: 5–6) argue that:

> It is this very emptiness ... that makes it so politically 'useful' and
> malleable a discourse for ideologues. The 'Other' – crucial to any
> form of identity but especially to such fuzzy ones – can be easily
> redefined, precisely because autochthony as such has hardly any
> substance.

It becomes a valuable asset for political entrepreneurs, and the very plasticity of the autochthony trope makes it attractive for rapidly changing situations where the identity of the 'other' (the 'allochton' or 'stranger' in the discursive cosmology of autochthony) is constantly changing. Moreover, it works to flatten other forms of difference, obscuring other forms of political hierarchies. As such, it is the suppleness that makes autochthony discourses an attractive resource for dealing with the rapidly accelerating flows of peoples, ideas and images. For many, autochthony functions as a useful tool for closure in the face of unrelenting and disruptive openness. It is also a seductive weapon for political entrepreneurs. Stephen Jackson (2006: 112) finds that the autochthony discourse offers local politicians in DRC a 'politically powerful multivalence' because it 'slyly speaks to multiple audiences simultaneously (while eliding the question of which allochthons, or from whose point of view)'.

Yet, in practice, the illusion of ontological certainty provided by the autochthony trope is repeatedly exposed as being just that, an illusion. Belonging is always relative, and being there 'first' is virtually impossible to prove. Thus, there is always the danger of being accused of being a 'fake' autochthon and not really belonging. The trope is highly unstable and slippery. Jackson refers to this as the 'nervous language' of autochthony. As he writes:

> Autochthony discourse is also endemically nervous because
> many of those deploying it suffer the nagging fear that they could
> suddenly find themselves its objects. At some level, no one in the
> DRC seems to be sufficiently autochthonous to escape at some
> point becoming the target for accusations of foreignness... The
> psychological state resulting from this instability is, by definition,
> paranoia. (ibid.: 115)

In many African contexts, the employment of the autochthony trope has led to what Geschiere and Jackson (2006: 6) call the 'segmentarising' tenor of these discourses: 'There seems to be an inherent tendency to define the "Other" at ever closer range; the concomitant danger is that someone can always claim to "belong" even more than you do.' We see this in Kenya in the case of political violence around Mount Elgon and, as Marshall-Fratani (2006: 37) notes with regards to Côte d'Ivoire, the 'war has shown that in the designation of political enemies and allies, ethnicity and autochthony prove to be highly unstable and deceptive'. The problem is that autochthony is always relative. It seems to promise some degree of security and certainty based on a truth claim uniting identity and space. Autoch-

thony's tragic irony is that employing the trope actually furthers the
ontological uncertainty it seeks to elide.

Autochthony and the production of violence

In their discussion of autochthony, Geschiere and Jackson (2006:
6) note that the 'naturalising' tenor of discourses on autochthony and
belonging is highly deceiving – this may also explain why it can so
easily have violent implications. It is this 'easy' connection between
autochthony and violence that we wish to explore a little further.
We suggest that there are at least three reasons why autochthony
discourses are often accompanied by violence.

First, as noted above, the certainty and security promised by the
primordial claims of autochthony are quickly exposed as illusions,
given the instability and plasticity of the trope. In seeking to shore
up the ontological foundations of one's truth claims, violence proves
to be a useful tool. Simply put, violence is a seductive provider of
ontological certainty. There are two points we wish to underscore
here. The first is the recognition that violence is part of a com-
municative strategy (Richards 1996; Appadurai 1999). The second is
the performative dimension of identity and the role that violence can
play. Subject formation is inherently liminal and unstable, especially
among the youth, and employing violent acts in the performance of
identity is both an act of empowerment and an attempt to secure a
foundation for truth claims.

Within autochthonous violence, there is an implicit discursive and
performative connection between clarity and purity. Appadurai has
drawn attention to the links between violence, purity and ontological
uncertainty in his discussion of ethnocide. He focuses on 'bodily
violence between actors with routine – and generally benign – prior
knowledge of one another' in order to 'illuminate "threshold" or
trigger conditions where managed or endemic social conflict gives
way to runaway violence'. In an unstable situation where violence
is 'explicitly about categories under stress and ideas striving for the
logic of self-evidence', the identification of the enemy demands fixed
criteria of classification and identification as well as taxonomical purity
(Appadurai 1999: 310). Appadurai suggests that this quest for purity
and clarity can trigger violence. Drawing upon Liisa Malkki's work on
Hutu refugees from Burundi, he argues that questions of identification
and knowledge of the ethnic body in that case lay at the heart of

the performance of violence. As Malkki (1995: 88) argues, 'through violence, bodies of individual persons become metamorphosed into specimens of the ethnic category for which they are supposed to stand'. The body functions as both a source of and a target for violence. The almost ritualistic forms of violence enacted upon bodies – from rape to mutilation – are seen as an integral part of a project to stabilise the body of the ethnic other, to eliminate impurities and reify boundaries. The body – especially the female body – becomes the site of violent closure in situations of categorical uncertainty and purification. Of course, violence ultimately fails to produce ontological certainty. As Marshall-Fratani (2006: 38) observes in the Côte d'Ivoire context:

> These brutal actions by no means establish certainty; indeed, they only exacerbate the frustrations of their perpetrators and lead to cycles of revenge and pre-emptive violence, as the on-going killings between autochthons and strangers testify.

This situation is mirrored in DRC, where Jackson (2006: 115) observes that the inherent paradox between autochthony as a powerful motivator and an empty trope 'dooms this violence to failure, but it is a failure made all the more violent because of its frustration'.

The second reason for suggesting an intimate relationship between violence and autochthony discourses is the observation that those discourses often rely on a narrative of victimisation. The stories told of the 'self' and 'other' are frequently cast not just as autochthon versus alien but also as victim versus aggressor. In numerous cases, political entrepreneurs have produced historical narratives of victimisation within their communities' collective memory, and have employed that memory as a justification for violence. Thus, one often finds a violent cycle of memory and counter-memory, where one remembered atrocity justifies another or, in some cases, a pre-emptive attack to thwart an expected atrocity built on the remembrance of past wrongdoings. For example, the portrayal of victimisation and its concomitant narrative of autochthonous 'revenge' has been a striking feature in the continuing conflict in Côte d'Ivoire. This is also readily apparent in the cases of Rwanda and the Congo, where memories of victimisation have been (and continue to be) crucial cognitive frames for those engaging in extreme forms of violence (Mamdani 2001; Dunn 2003; Turner 2007).

The employment of a historical narrative of violent victimisation is often utilised to legitimise the use of violence. Here it is useful to remember the observations of Frantz Fanon (1965) and his advocacy of violence to cleanse and restore the psyche of the colonial victim. The reference to Fanon is particularly significant given that the old imaginaries of revolution, national liberation, anti-imperialism, and nativism have been reactivated by the youth. As Mbembe (2001: 36) notes:

> Under the flashy rags of the current international lexicon (democracy, social movements, civil society) these imaginaries now combine in opposition to globalisation, reactivating the metaphysics of difference, re-enchanting tradition and reviving the utopia of an Africa cut off from the rest of the world and de-occidentalised.

Together with the redeployment of revolutionary, anti-imperial narratives built on historical memories of violent victimisation comes an often explicit legitimisation of violence against the 'aliens' and the 'invaders'. In the case of Côte d'Ivoire, the Jeunes Patriotes ideologues often referred to their 'struggle' against people defined as 'aliens' and 'invaders' as 'the second war of liberation' – a most useful rhetorical tactic, but completely ignoring the fact that a 'first war of liberation' never actually took place.

A third reason for the intimate relationship between violence and autochthony discourses can be found in the processes of state-making. Appadurai (1999: 318) observes that:

> In no case of ethnocide of which we have knowledge can it be shown that these categories are innocent of state practices (usually through the census and often involving crucial forms of welfare or potential punishment).

Violence in its various manifestations is at the very core of statecraft. The desire for closure, reification and concretisation invokes practices of coding and overcoding, territorialising and re-territorialising, and other forms of structural violence. As Doty (2003: 13) notes: 'Any practice of statecraft, any movement toward the never fully realized or realizable concretization of this abstract ideal is inextricably linked with violence.' But this violence is not exclusively structural, as those engaging in violent articulations of autochthony and anti-immigrant discourses clearly demonstrate. The desire for order – a desire at the heart of state-making processes – invokes manifestations of violence in multiple forms.

The processes of state-making rest on decoding and recoding space and identity: inside/outside and native/stranger. It is important to recognise that state-making processes are invoked and performed by multiple actors, not just official state agents. In each case of autochthonous violence in Africa, groups and individuals employing autochthony discourses are engaged in the production of political identities as part of a state-making process. These knowledges are played out on the body of the victims:

> The maiming and mutilation of ethnicised bodies is a desperate
> effort to restore the validity of somatic markers of 'otherness' in
> the face of the uncertainties posed by census labels, demographic
> shifts, and linguistic changes, all of which make ethnic affiliations
> less somatic and bodily, more social and elective. (Appadurai 1999:
> 320)

The representation and presence of the alien/stranger are cornerstone aspects of state-making processes, and invoking the threat the aliens pose to the social order can necessitate violent manifestations of the state and of state-making processes. In parts of Africa, the central government may be institutionally weak, but that does not mean that state-making processes are not highly active.

Conclusion

We suggest that autochthonous violence is an effect of, rather than merely a reaction to, contemporary trends of globalisation and state-making. Some have suggested that the state has been weakened by these global processes and autochthonous violence occurs in the vacuum left by the collapsed or failed state. But such arguments misread the ways in which state-making processes have adapted to globalisation. In his examination of autochthony in the Kenyan case, John Lonsdale (2008a: 311–12) offers an insightful intervention that is worth quoting at length:

> The opportunities and threats of globalisation may also have
> stimulated a tighter sense of belonging, but it is important to get
> that argument straight. Globalisation can well be said to have given
> birth to modern states and the international system. But globalisa-
> tion is not a general phenomenon. It takes specific local forms. In
> Africa, it can teach the states it has spawned to become predators,

reaching out to them with the tight fist of mafia capitalism as much as with the market's open, allegedly fertile, hand. It is not to guard against some existential global threat that Africans expel stranger neighbours from the local community. They rebel, rather, against the daily inequalities, the unpredictable inclusions and exclusions by which their states decide who is to gain from global linkages, and who bear their local costs.

Thus, we need to re-insert the state into examinations of autochthony, not merely as an institution but also as a political arena, a discursive space, and a process in which there are 'winners' and 'losers'.

The state functions as a privileged discursive space where political identities are produced and reproduced. As the cases discussed at the start of this chapter indicate, groups seek control over the apparatuses of the state not merely because they provide access to resources, but because they also have tremendous productive discursive power. For example, debates over citizenship laws underscore the power of the ethnographic state, where a state's claim to sovereignty creates for itself a privileged role in producing and controlling territorialised political spaces and identities. As Ruth Marshall-Fratani (2006: 11) has argued: 'What is at stake in the current Ivorian crisis is not only a struggle for state power, but also, and more importantly, the redefinition of the content of citizenship and the conditions of sovereignty.' Like other autochthony conflicts, it is a war about borders, crystallising liminal spaces and social categories and practices, with the state as the privileged discursive space where power is produced within state-making practices.

The autochthony trope appears not in the absence of the state, but as an integral part of state-making practices. Given the increasing intensity of ontological uncertainty that pervades the current post-colonial condition, the employment of autochthony discourses resonates deeply with populations longing for a sense of primal security and certainty. And while this sense of security is inevitably fleeting, given the instability and plasticity of the trope, we suspect it will remain a significant part of the political landscape – in Africa and elsewhere – for some time to come because of its attractive and seemingly self-evident logic.

3 | LIBERIA: CIVIL WAR AND THE 'MANDINGO QUESTION'

Liberia has a long and complicated history. During the period from 1980 to 2003, Liberia become synonymous with war, chaos and destruction. The underlying causes of conflict, however, are deeply entrenched in Liberian history. Even if the word 'autochthony' has not been part of the Liberian discourse, the same debate that we find in countries such as Côte d'Ivoire and DRC has been an integral aspect of daily life and politics in Liberia.

Liberia consists of sixteen major groups of people, each possessing its own traditions, customs, religious philosophies, languages and dialects. In order to understand the history of state formation in Liberia, we must also take into consideration the group of freed slaves repatriated from the United States between 1822 and 1861 to this part of the West African coast. In 1847, these freed slaves established the Republic of Liberia and became known as the Americo-Liberians. The intention was to create a safe haven for freed slaves; the problem, however, was that they were just as much strangers in Liberia as they had been in the United States. Given a land to govern, they built their system of rule on the only political and administrative system with which they were familiar: the system of the plantations in the Deep South of the United States. The main difference, of course, was that this time they were the 'masters' and the indigenous people the 'servants'. Trapped within this model, they embarked on a political strategy of division between the 'self' (perceived as the civilised, educated class) and the 'other' (perceived as the savage, a native underclass to be kept in place by hard work and discipline) (see Ellis 1999; Bøås 2005).

When the Republic of Liberia was established in 1847, a constitution based on the American model was adopted. According to the Liberian constitution, all men are born equally free and independent and have certain natural, inherent and inalienable rights. However, 'all men' did not mean all men who inhabited the area to which the constitution laid claim; on the contrary, the constitution strongly differentiated between the repatriates and the indigenous population. The members of the so-called 'native tribes' were not eligible for election or voting. A firm division between these two groups was therefore institutionalised, laying the foundation for entrenched aliena-tion between the different ethnic groups in Liberia, and between these groups and the new upper class comprised of the Americo-Liberians. In 1870, the True Whig Party (TWP) was established, and for the next 110 years Liberia was a de facto one-party state (Bøås 2005).

By the early 1920s, the Americo-Liberian elite had secured its rule through a combination of force and clientelistic arrangements. A complex system of pyramidal patron–client relationships throughout Liberian society, with the Americo-Liberian elite at the top, maintained what must be characterised as 'settler rule' (Ellis 1999). This system remained more or less in place until riots broke out in April 1979 against President William Tolbert and his regime. Trying to secure his position, Tolbert declared a state of emergency and put down the riots with full force. Most leaders of the small and fragmented opposition parties that had emerged under his rule were arrested. However, only two days before their cases were due to appear in court, a group of seventeen enlisted men killed Tolbert, overthrew the government and executed several of the ministers on the beach in Monrovia. The majority of the population interpreted the removal from power of the TWP regime as a blessing, and many envisioned a new era for Liberia in which finally 'all men would be equal'.

It soon became obvious, however, that the soldiers, under the leadership of Samuel Doe, were not able or willing to even attempt to reform the Liberian state. On the contrary, they themselves became captives of the predatory logic of the state that the Americo-Liberian elite had established. Doe's almost ten years in power are a story of petty corruption, grand theft of state resources, murder, rape, torture and other human rights abuses. As social tensions increased, the country was ripe for a civil war – a war that started on Christmas Eve 1989 when the National Patriotic Front of Liberia (NPFL), a small rebel army led by Charles Taylor, crossed the border into Liberia from Côte d'Ivoire (Bøås 2005).

No one knows how many people died in the first part of the Lib-erian civil war (1990–97); some say 60,000 while others claim casual-ties as high as 250,000. The first estimate is probably more realistic than the latter. What is clear, however, is that the level of human suffering created by the war was enormous, and the war also spilled over to other West African countries. Consequences of the Liberian civil war – including refugee flows, political and economic destabilisation, the creation of new military alliances and their incorporation into the underground economy of the Liberian civil war – could be identified in Burkina Faso, Côte d'Ivoire, Guinea-Bissau, Guinea, Nigeria and, of course, Sierra Leone.

Between 1994 and 1996, several attempts to implement a peace agreement in Liberia failed, mainly because of the unwillingness of Nigeria to accept a deal that included Charles Taylor. In 1996, however, Taylor and the then Nigerian ruler Sani Abacha reached an agreement, and elections were held in July 1996. In relatively free and fair elections supervised by international election observers, Taylor won about 75 per cent of the votes. The main reason for this was that Taylor's movement was the best organised and the most ethnically diverse of the armed factions, and the civilian opposition was too fragmented and disorganised to put up a real challenge to him.

Once in power, Taylor and his entourage exploited their powerful positions and pre-war political networks to commandeer resources that they already managed. They also proceeded to hollow out the state, siphoning off resources and shrinking the armed forces. Dismissing around 2,500 personnel (mostly ethnic Krahn), Taylor relied on his Anti-Terrorist Unit as a private militia. In a continent known for neopatrimonialism and personal rule, Taylor's regime became distinguished for its extreme personalisation of authority.

As William Reno (2007: 71) observed:

> Liberia under Taylor was as a prime example of a system of personal rule constructed behind a façade of statehood. This system of authority is founded on the ability of the ruler to control his subordinates' access to markets. Control over a state and the prerogatives of sovereignty that global recognition accords gives the ruler the authority to manipulate laws and regulations to favor his associates... In its more extreme forms in places like Taylor's Liberia, rulers end up controlling people and building political networks through domination of markets, not the expensive and potentially dangerous institutions of a functioning bureaucratic state.

It is within this context that the civil war restarted. The Mano

River region was increasingly characterised by informal political net-works of powerful individuals, clandestine cross-border commercial and political ties, and veteran senior fighters moving freely between neighbouring countries.

However, from 1997 to 2000, the situation in most parts of Liberia was relatively calm, but, in the northern territory of Lofa County, instability and low-level conflict continued and by 1999 the second phase of the Liberian civil war was well on its way. Three years later, Taylor's enemies in the rebel factions Liberians United for Reconcili-ation and Democracy (LURD) and the Movement for Democracy in Liberia (MODEL) had brought the war back to Monrovia.

LURD was formally founded in a meeting in Freetown, Sierra Leone in February 2000. The coalition was made up largely of a collection of politicians and former fighters who resented (and failed to profit from) Taylor's manipulation of the 1995 Abuja Agreement that ended the first phase of Liberia's civil war. After his victory, Taylor had systematically targeted his wartime rivals and political opponents. On 18 September 1998, at least several hundred members of the United Liberation Movement of Liberia for Democracy-Johnson faction (ULIMO-J), Taylor's main opponents during the 1989–95 phase of Liberia's war, were murdered in what became known as the Camp Johnson Road incident. The newly formed LURD coalition thus had plenty of groups of aggrieved former combatants to draw on. A number of these groups enjoyed foreign patronage. For example, LURD was supported by Guinea's President Conté, who resented Taylor's attempt to destabilise his own country, and MODEL was supported by Côte d'Ivoire's President Gbagbo.

LURD began a serious campaign of fighting in Lofa County starting on 8 July 2000, soon leading to the capture of Voinjama, the county headquarters. The fighting in Lofa was particularly brutal and LURD was accused of engaging in serious human rights violations (ICG 2003: 9). The Liberian government also claimed that LURD was involved in a series of cross-border raids into Guinea, but it is more likely that those attacks were carried out by Liberian army units and militias that were supporting a new insurgent group, the Rassemblement des Forces Démocratiques de Guinée (RFDG). Reno (2007: 73–6) has suggested that Taylor actively enhanced LURD's reputation as part of his own political strategy, part of which was to develop a cover for shipping men and arms to Lofa County to support the Revolutionary United Front (RUF) in neighbouring Sierra Leone. If an RUF government could be established in Sierra Leone as part of a peace agreement (as his own NPFL had done), Taylor's diplomatic isolation would have lessened and it would have left his entourage in possession of a lucrative commercial network that was critical to their political strategies.

Yet, by 2001, the RUF was in the process of being defeated by British and United Nations (UN) military offensives. As Taylor's Sierra Leone allies' troubles increased, LURD launched more concerted offensives. By February 2002, LURD was driving deeper into Liberia along the Sierra Leone border. LURD's military successes led many to suspect that they were being assisted by British and/or American officials (ICG 2003: 3; Reno 2007). By the next year, LURD controlled major highway junctions outside Monrovia, cutting Taylor's forces from their rear bases. Despite these advances, they were unable to take Monrovia and unseat Taylor. Increasingly they turned to international negotiators to convince Taylor to seek exile. Taylor finally left Liberia on 11 August 2003, accepting exile in Nigeria. But this had far less to do with LURD's military advances than with a promise made by an international contact group, which included US, British and French officials, that he would not be prosecuted before a war crimes tribunal in Sierra Leone if he left Monrovia. While secret at the time, in March the UN-sanctioned war crimes tribunal had issued an indictment of Taylor, accusing him of crimes against humanity for his aid to the RUF (Special Court for Sierra Leone, 2003). In 2012 Taylor was finally sentenced to fifty years in prison by the Special Court for Sierra Leone, but it is of significant interest to note that, even if the sentence means that Taylor will have to spend the rest of his life in prison, the court nonetheless dismissed the theory that Taylor was the kingpin in a joint criminal enterprise that had been behind the war in Sierra Leone (and Liberia).

In August 2003, Liberia thus emerged from a devastating fourteen years of civil war with almost every single institution and piece of infrastructure broken and bent. When Taylor went into exile, power was first transferred to his vice-president Moses Blah before the National Transitional Government of Liberia (NTGL) was established under the leadership of Gyude Bryant to steer Liberia through the two-year transition phase agreed upon in the Comprehensive Peace Agreement (CPA). Together with the UN Mission in Liberia (UNMIL), the

NTGL managed to conduct the relatively free and fair elections in the autumn of 2005 that brought Ellen Johnson Sirleaf to power, but this transition period also created new problems and challenges that continue to haunt Liberia. Ellen Johnson Sirleaf was re-elected in 2011, but even if this election continued her rule, the boycott by the opposition clearly demonstrated that the cleavages that became violently manifest during the civil war still exist in Liberia (Bøås and Utas 2013).

The main problem was the composition of the NTGL. It was not much different from previous power-sharing arrangements. Like previous Liberian governments, the NTGL was basically a highly competitive patrimonial environment where various elites were locked into struggles over state resources. A few representatives from the private sector and civil society were included in the NTGL, but by and large the transitional government reflected the prevailing military power balance between the three main factions – Taylor's government army, LURD and MODEL – meaning that the real powers in the NTGL were the members of the former warring factions (Bøås 2009c).

LURD and MODEL had won the war but there was no way that these groups could win the peace. LURD was a Mandingo-dominated group that would never be able to win a national election. The Krahn, on the other hand, are also a relatively small group, and they are also still marked by the fact that many other Liberians believe that they were the favoured group during Samuel Doe's dictatorship. Their interest in the NTGL was therefore not in the transition as such. Rather, it represented a last chance of enrichment before multiparty elections would blow them into oblivion. Acutely aware of this, faction leaders even openly traded in NTGL positions, selling them to the highest bidder. This is the legacy that Ellen Johnson Sirleaf's government is still struggling with as she enters her second term in office.

State institutions have been reconstructed, but they are far from functioning optimally. Liberian courts are still short of judges, particularly outside Monrovia. Police reform has been implemented, but while the uniforms are new, many Liberians do not believe that much else has changed. Petty corruption by members of the police force is still prevalent – one major reason is the lack of pay. Often the policeman or -woman on duty is not paid to be on duty, but rather he or she is paying someone higher up in order to be allowed to be on duty that particular day at that particular market. Education and other social services (such as hospitals and health clinics) are in the process of being rebuilt, but such services come at a cost (formal and informal) and the quality is generally low. As many parents see it, particularly in the rural areas, why bother sending your kids to school when they learn next to nothing as the teacher cannot read or write properly either and school books are few, old and usually of low quality? These issues are part and parcel of Liberian politics and society and integrally linked to difficult questions of rights and belonging. Nowhere is this more evident that in the northernmost Liberian county of Lofa.

Lofa County

Lofa is the northernmost Liberian county, and Voinjama is the largest city and county capital. Although Kissi, Kpelle and Mano communities also live in Lofa, the two main ethnic groups are the Loma and the Mandingo. The cultivation of upland rice is the most important agricultural activity for both the Loma and the Mandingo. Rice is their staple food and the mode of production is swidden agriculture (or slash-and-burn), in which fallow periods vary from four to twelve years depending on factors such as population density, land availability and soil fertility. This suggests that each household needs access to large areas of land (Højbjerg 2007). Parts of Lofa may seem sparsely populated and land therefore abundant, but this is not necessarily the case. At times, land may be a scarce commodity, and we have to bear in mind that land is also the most essential element of rural life. Land is everything: belonging to the land is what guarantees the rights of present as well as future generations, and while citizenship does not in itself guarantee the right to land, at the very least it allows those who are citizens to enter the political economy of land and questions of land rights (Mamdani 2002). Thus, there is a direct link between contested citizenship and land rights issues.

The political affairs of Lofa have always been a world apart from Monrovia and Central Liberia, but, nevertheless, the county was swiftly integrated into the Liberian civil war. This was partly due to the dynamics of the war, but also due to pre-existing tensions between the Loma, who consider themselves autochthonous to the area, and the Mandingo, who generally are seen as latecomers and immigrants.[1] The Mandingo are not considered proper Liberians, but as a people of foreign origin (Bøås 2005; Konneh 1996). The implication is that their very right to be considered Liberian citizens is often questioned when conflicts occur between people of Mandingo origin and those belonging to other ethnic groups. Thus, 'the other indigenous ethnic groups put them in essentially the same "foreigners category" as the Settlers; that is, the Mandingo are viewed as "foreigners" from Guinea – not real Liberians' (Konneh 1996).

Consequently, the relationship between the two main ethnic groups in Lofa has been tense and hostile, particularly since the beginning of the civil war in 1989–90. The Mandingo accuse the Loma of supporting Taylor's forces when they reached this part of Liberia in the autumn of 1990, whereas the Loma believe that the attacks in 1992 on their towns by the Mandingo militia (ULIMO)[2] were unjustified and mainly carried out to take their land and steal their belongings. Similar views emerged when LURD crossed over the border from Guinea in 1998–99. The Loma claim that LURD forces – also a Mandingo-dominated movement – attacked their villages indiscriminately.[3]

The same conflict pattern also came to the fore during the elections in October and November 2005. In the first round of the presidential elections, the Mandingo voted for their candidate, the former warlord Alhaji Kromah, and his All Liberian Coalition Party (ALCOP). In the Mandingo towns along the border with Guinea, Kromah received over 95 per cent of the votes. However, as the Mandingo constitute a majority in only a few places in Lofa, mainly along the border, Kromah received only 18 per cent of the total votes in the county, taking him to second place in the first presidential round in Lofa. The main reason for the Mandingo support of Kromah was that they saw the former warlord as a hero; a friend of the Mandingo nation who defended them not only against Taylor's forces but also against the Loma (Bøås and Hatløy 2008).

In the collective memory of the Mandingo, massacres such as the one in Bakiedou in 1990 and the wartime destruction of their mosques are very much alive and have created their own melancholic tunes of uncertainty and insecurity. These are not manifested in despair, but in a dual sense of ethnic solidarity and uncertainty – given the fact that their overall position in the Liberian polity is contested. This is an integral part of their daily discourse. The war, in the form of physical destruction as well as in terms of memory and identity, is still present in Lofa. This is vividly illustrated by the death and burial in the spring of 2007 of Philip Kamara and Aliyu Sheriff, two leading LURD commanders. They died of natural causes, but on their death they were praised as true Mandingo warriors: the defenders of the Mandingo nation in Liberia. Receiving the highest honour the Mandingo of Liberia can give to their deceased sons, they were buried in the heart of their respective towns together with the founding fathers of the Mandingo nation. Philip Kamara's grave in Sakomedu is next to the grave of the legendary Chief Bongo, and Aliyu Sheriff's grave is next to those of the founding fathers of Bakiedou, the oldest Mandingo settlement in Lofa. No one else has ever been judged worthy of being buried next to Chief Bongo, and, according to Sheriff's father, this was the first time in more than eighty years that a new grave had been made in the heart of Bakiedou.

The massive turnout at their burials not only suggests that the LURD network is still intact, but, more significantly, the position that these two former warlords have in the Mandingo imaginary. They were not putting a feared warlord into his shallow grave; they were conducting a funeral for a friend. During the night of their burials, tales of the plight of the Mandingo were retold once more as female relatives wept over the loss of their beloved sons. In Monrovia or in the Loma communities in Lofa, few felt anything but relief when the news broke that Sheriff had died, the man who had sent wave after wave of grenades into Monrovia during the LURD offensive in the summer of 2003. Outside their community, both Kamara and Sheriff were seen as hard and dangerous men that one would cross at one's own peril. One man's friend is another man's enemy, and, as elsewhere, the reason for this is embedded in history and the tales of origin that divide societies (see Bøås 2009b).

Lofa tales of origin

The origin of the Loma and Mandingo of Lofa is, if not lost in history, at least uncertain. What we do know is that this area of Liberia, far from being an isolated tribal setting, has been a dynamic theatre where there has been a continuous flux of heterogeneous people over the past four or five centuries (D'Azevedo 1962). It is a history of warfare, shifting alliances and competition for control over trade routes. Historically it has been a multicultural and politically diverse region, which suggests that, in objective terms, the current ethnic groups are more a consequence of 'state-building' than historically coherent groups with a common distant past. Be that as it may, what is important for our purposes is not what is historically correct (if anybody can really tell) but the meta-narratives on which current groups in conflict base their collective memories.

According to Loma folklore, the place of origin of their founding ancestors is the savannah area in the Beyla region in Guinea. From this place, an invading enemy gradually pushed them into the Guinean–Liberian forest zone. This may have been the Mande invasion in the sixteenth century. Whether or not this is the case, more noteworthy is the fact that most of the Loma founding narratives connect the origin of the Loma to that of the Konianké, the Guinean version of the Liberian Mandingo. According to this history, they were initially the same. The story centres on Fala Wubo – here presented as the original ancestor of the Loma. When faced with the overwhelming force of an invading army in the Beyla region, Fala Wubo and his sons trekked to the area between Macenta and Voinjama (the current border area between Liberia and Guinea), defeated the people who lived there and established a chiefdom and the predecessor of the Loma version of the Poro society.[4]

Fala Wubo also had a brother named Seimavileh who refused to join the Poro society established by Fala Wubo. According to the tale of the Loma, Seimavileh is the forefather of the Mandingo of Lofa. The Mandingo tell a similar story, but in their version their ancestor's name is Foningama (or sometimes Feren Kamara). The Mandingo story is therefore both similar and slightly different to the one told by the Loma. However, for both the Loma and the Mandingo, this tale of conflict between ancestors is also seen as the beginning of a long history of co-operation as well as conflict – a history firmly tied to the 'stranger-father' institution (elaborated in the next section of this chapter) that is supposed to regulate local land politics between 'first-comers' and 'latecomers' in this part of Liberia.

Although the Mandingo generally accept the Loma as the autochthonous first-comers, this is not the end of the debate; their relationship is also affected by the coming of the modern state system. Liberian state control of Lofa was effected only a long time after the Mandingo moved into this area. It was as late as 1911 that the Liberian army was sent to Lofa to establish state control, and it was not until the 1920s that the area was considered safe for travel. The issue of demarcating the border between Liberia and the French colony of Guinea was not settled until 1928. In the Mandingo narrative of the making of the Liberian state, it is their legendary Chief Bongo who settled the border issue by deciding that his people should belong to Liberia and not to French Guinea. In this way, the Mandingo connect their claim to Liberian citizenship and autochthony to the very construction of the Liberian state, arguing that if it had not been for their powerful chief, this part of Lofa would have been ruled from Conakry. This story was basically ignored at that time and it is still contested today. Most Loma refuse to believe that Chief Bongo was as powerful as the Mandingo claim. However, it is very likely that Bongo was a powerful chief and warrior, and as French colonial control of the Guinée Forestière region was weak, his actions and decisions may have had an impact on these events. But this did not improve the position of the Mandingo. It was not until the beginning of the 1940s that they were granted full citizenship in Liberia, mainly in order to prove the effectiveness of the Liberian state's control of the border area (Liebenow 1987).

Autochthonous 'stranger-father' relations[5]

The Loma and the Mandingo may or may not share a mutual origin, but it is only partly useful understanding their ethnogenesis. They have lived together for a considerable amount of time, but their relationship is also conflictual and their coexistence segmented. When the Loma and the Mandingo inhabit the same town or village, they almost always live in distinct quarters of the town. In a majority Loma town with a Mandingo minority population, there will be a separate Mandingo section of the town, which is clearly demarcated from the rest. The Mandingo section will have a Mandingo chief who rules his section, but who in town affairs will be subordinate to the Loma chief. This is not unique to the relationship between the Loma and the Mandingo. What it shows is how immensely hierarchical these societies are (see also Murphy 1980).

Even in homogeneous Loma or Mandingo villages, there are always some lineages that claim to be more autochthonous than others. There is always a narrative about a forefather or ancestor – the man and the family who originally established the village. And those who can trace their belonging back to this forefather will have certain inalienable rights that others do not necessarily have. This will be the ruling lineage. In the case of the original Mandingo villages in the Voinjama District of Lofa along the Guinea border (such as Bakiedou,

Sakomedu and Tusso), the ruling lineages are those that can trace their belonging back to the village founding fathers buried in the heart (e.g. the middle) of the town. This hierarchical stratification of rights is further extended in villages that also harbour residents from other ethnic groups, such as the mixed towns in Lofa with a Mandingo minority and a Loma majority.

It is precisely at this point that the institution of 'stranger-father' relationships enters into the equation. When the Mandingo first arrived in Lofa it was most often as individual traders conducting long-distance commerce between the forest areas of Liberia and the savannah regions further inland, bringing with them both much needed goods and important skills such as blacksmithing. In many ways, the first Mandingo settlers must have had access to greater economic resources than the original Loma inhabitants. However, in order to settle permanently and gain access to land, the Mandingo had to enter into subordinate alliances through the 'stranger-father' institution. In basic terms, this means that a 'stranger' who seeks to settle in a village or community needs to be adopted by an autochthonous 'father'. The stranger must have a father – a figure of authority who takes upon himself the responsibility of ensuring that the stranger behaves in accordance with the rules and regulations of the community. For example, when a Mandingo first moved into a Loma town, he also entered into a subordinate position with a 'stranger-father', locking himself and his lineage into a subordinate political position forever with regard to decisions about land and land use. The result of this interaction was that notions of political alignment in local everyday politics were relatively fixed, creating a hierarchical political system that was supposed to regulate titles to land.

With the creation of Liberian state land tenure, however, came a complex cocktail of socially and politically embedded rights that were negotiated in dynamic relationships between and among different groups of people and the Liberian state. A dual land tenure system was established in Liberia (and still exists), where the government recognised both deeded ownership and customary users' rights. All undeeded land is also public land, including land held under the customary system. However, both individuals and groups of people who live under customary law can apply to have their land surveyed and protected by a deed through the Government Land Commissioner operating in their county.

In practice, what this means is that the right to land is closely connected to membership of a specific group, be it the nuclear or extended family, the larger descent group or the ethnic group, and to the various relationships of those groups to modern property regimes. Land rights are therefore often contested, always negotiable, and change over time. The only thing that is constant is that membership of a group and recognised 'citizenship' in a geographical area are essential in these processes. Land rights issues are therefore particularly vulnerable to the politics of identity and belonging, and one important asset in such situations is the ability to stake your claim to land from the position of being autochthonous, for example as a 'son of the soil', whereas your counterpart is presented as a 'newcomer', an 'immigrant' or a 'stranger'. In such cases, claiming citizenship within the community, area or nation is of primary importance because, although it does not entitle you to resources, it at least entitles you to enter the struggle for them.

In Lofa, as in most other places in Liberia, everybody who is allowed to stay in a village is allocated some land for food crop production (although the size of the plots and their number may vary greatly), but only those defined as autochthonous or 'sons of the soil' were originally allowed to cultivate so-called life crops (for example, tree crops such as rubber, cocoa, coffee and banana). By cultivating tree crops one also embeds oneself in the soil and makes a permanent connection to it. In order to be considered autochthonous, being a first-comer is a necessary, but not the only, criterion; one must also transform the landscape permanently from wilderness to a field for one's livelihood. This can only be achieved by planting life crops. Part of the 'bad blood' between the Loma and the Mandingo in Lofa, which Taylor's forces so cunningly used to their advantage during the war, was that some Mandingo either had taken or been given the right to cultivate life crops through their position as providers of rural credit in towns where they constituted a minority. It should be noted that even if the Mandingo were politically marginalised through the 'stranger-father' institution, they represented economic muscle through their access to Mandingo trade networks.

The contested practices of marriage and marriage alliances also revolve around similar issues. Formally the Mandingo are politically subordinate, but, as has already been suggested, formal subordination can easily be offset by economic might. Alliance by marriage is an important aspect of local land politics in Lofa, and the Mandingo have undoubtedly used their economic position to build alliances by marrying Loma women from land-ruling lineages. However, as they also seek to protect their group identity (for trading as well as for religious purposes), they effectively discourage their daughters from marrying into Loma lineages, if not openly refusing such marriages. As a result, they are perceived as seeking a permanent position by being 'wife-receivers' in the system of asymmetric marriage alliances that dominates in Lofa County (see Temin 2004; Richards et al. 2005). These tensions are not a creation of the war. Rather, they represent a controversial issue deeply embedded in history, but made much worse by the war and the massive levels of displacement that followed in its wake.

One consequence was that, in the immediate pre-war situation in Lofa, part of the local Loma discourse on the Mandingo centred on how the latter had upset the balance, disturbing certain rights seen as inalienable. Indeed, in one community near Voinjama, a group of Mandingo were accused of having used unpaid credit to force through an arrangement that implied that they had established a farm in a 'forbidden forest' reserved for the Sande (the female variant of the male Poro). Therefore, when the war came to Lofa, sections of the autochthonous population used it to reclaim what they believed were their natural rights. Viewed in this manner, the warlords, the grand plans, the elites and the international connections become less important. What we are left with is the intertwining of a series of local conflicts embedded within a larger pattern of warfare, as local communities – dazzled and confused by these very same events – tried to protect as well as reclaim what they believed belonged to them. The outcome was not pretty; moreover, this also creates a pattern of war that is not easily broken. This was the context that propelled men such as Philip Kamara and Aliyu Sheriff into the positions that they came to occupy during the war.

Post-war challenges

As we have seen already, in the 2005 presidential elections the Mandingo voted for their candidate, the former warlord Alhaji Kromah and his ALCOP. The key point is that the Mandingo do not see Kromah and his commanders (such as Kamara and Sheriff) as criminal warlords but as those who defended them, not only against

Taylor's forces but also against his allies among the Loma.[6] Kromah
is one of their own, a true friend and a 'son of the soil', whereas
this segment of the Liberian electorate sees Ellen Johnson Sirleaf as
a former ally of Taylor. At the beginning of the war, Johnson Sirleaf
supported Taylor for a short while, and therefore, as the Mandingo
understand their recent history, she also shares some blame for their
suffering. In the Mandingo meta-narrative, the massacres at Bakiedou
and other places and the burning of their mosques and villages are
still very much alive.[7] Their sense of ethnic solidarity, based on mutual
uncertainty as their position in Liberia is questioned and contested,
may yet turn parts of Liberia into conflict zones once more.

The return process also complicated the situation. As we see from
Figure 3.1, the Mandingo were the first to return after the war: more
than 70 per cent went back to Lofa in 2004, whereas only 34 per cent
of the Loma and 14 per cent of the Kpelle returned that year. The
reason for this is very simple. Lofa County, and in particular Voinjama
District, was controlled by LURD when the war ended. LURD was
by and large a Mandingo insurgency, thus making people belonging
to this group the majority among the early returnees. They settled
on their original land, for instance in the old Mandingo towns along
the Guinean border (i.e. Bakiedou, Sakomedu and Tusso), but also
in houses and on land that once, and sometimes for nearly fifteen
years previously, had belonged to the Loma. This happened in some
of the mixed villages (i.e. Kugbemai and Vonema) where the Mandingo
constituted a minority population before the war started, but also
in Voinjama City itself. The early return of the Mandingo clearly
complicated the post-war situation in Lofa, and many of these land
rights conflicts still remain unresolved. However, the repercussions
have been less violent than in the Ganta area in Nimba County. The
main reason for this relates to the population pattern. Lofa is divided
into an eastern and a western part by the highway from Gbarnga to
Voinjama, which also passes through Zorzor. The Mandingo predomin-
antly live on the eastern side of Voinjama District, while the towns
on the north-western side tend to be Loma settlements. The main
exceptions are the mixed villages of Kugbemai and Vonema that lie
directly north of Voinjama City. The same is the case for a few towns
in Zorzor District that lie close to the highway mentioned above.

In the post-war period, this population pattern has been a blessing
for Lofa. The fact that the two main groups do not live too close to each

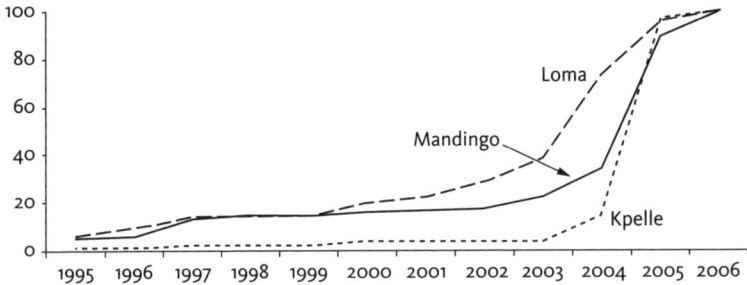

3.1 Returnees after the war, by group and by year (per cent)[8]

other may have spared Lofa from the high tension that characterises the situation between the Mandingo and the Gio and Mano in Ganta. The danger, however, is if the situation in Ganta should escalate out of control. This may cause so much concern among the Mandingo in Lofa that they might start to interpret the Ganta situation as a direct threat to their right to be regarded as Liberian citizens.[9] This could constitute the starting point of a new Mandingo insurgency.

Just like Voinjama, Ganta is an important border town, a centre for trade and commerce with Guinea. Ganta was also occupied by LURD, but only briefly. As LURD continued towards Gbarnga and Monrovia, the town was recaptured by pro-Taylor militias (consisting mainly of Gio and Mano youths). The first to return were therefore the Gio and Mano, who took advantage of the absence of the Mandingo not only to occupy their land but also to control the trade between Guinea, Ganta and Monrovia. What is happening in Ganta is therefore not only a land rights conflict, but also an attempt by Gio and Mano groups to break what they perceive as a Mandingo trade monopoly.[10] These new gains are protected by youth militias whose objective and sole purpose is to keep the Mandingo away from their property and 'convince' them that they should remain in Guinea.

Local interpretations of recent events are intertwined with collective historical memories. In Lofa, the Loma still tell tales about the *keele-kek koi*, the 'rolling war', which for them is their story of Mandingo intrusion and conquest of Loma territory. This invasion was not linked to the spread of Islam, as some evangelical churches argue today, but rather to the control of the trade routes linking the coastal areas with the interior, cutting across Lofa in a north–south direction. These trade routes are older than Liberia and the coming of the Americo-Liberians, but the foundation of Monrovia in 1820 certainly added to their importance and therefore also to the desire to control them. This was the backbone of the establishment of an economic alliance between the Mandingo and the Liberian state, first represented by Americo-Liberian rule and later by Samuel Doe's regime. This must have increased the sense of security among the Mandingo, a minority group, but it also made them a likely target if a revolt against state power should take place.

This is precisely what happened in 1990. Taylor's war and rule brought an end to this alliance, and Gio and Mano groups in Ganta are striving to keep it this way. The return of the Mandingo is unwanted because the Gio and Mano fear that this will once more result in the Mandingo having control over these trading routes. As such, the problem in Ganta is a local one, without any direct connection to the situation in Lofa. If it gets out of hand, however, the combined power of Mandingo solidarity and uncertainty may lead the people of Mandingo towns in Lofa (e.g. Bakiedou, Sakomedu, Tusso and others) who stood in the front line of the ULIMO/LURD struggle to question once more their position in Liberia, and to rearm. If this happens, yet another chapter may have to be written in the history of the Liberian civil war.

This is further exacerbated by the fact that renewed tensions in these hinterlands of Liberia could easily become tangled up with similar issues in the Guinée Forestière region of Guinea as well as with the evolving crisis of Condé's regime.[11] Some former LURD fighters have already drifted back into Guinea. Their exact number is unknown, but among this group there are people with a well-developed sense of history and purpose. They know very well that, just like Samory Touré's empire, LURD emerged from the forest-savannah frontier in Macenta Prefecture in Guinée Forestière.[12] Part of their meta-narrative is not only Mandingo insecurity in Liberia, but also the similar plight of their brethren, the Konianké in Guinea, and how the reconstitution of the 'glorious' Mandingo empire could redeem them from this insecurity.

A funeral for a friend – some concluding comments

Autochthony is just a word for a certain way of framing political debates, and although the word has not been part of the Liberian discourse, we see striking similarities between Liberia and the other cases examined in this book. There are commonalities that can best be described as 'tales of origin as political cleavage': in this case, competing tales of origin that challenge and oppose categories of 'first-comer' and 'latecomer'. The Mandingo story of Chief Bongo clearly establishes a counter-narrative to Loma claims to the status of autochthonous, and suggests that the struggle between first-comers and latecomers was substantially affected and even altered by the making of the modern state system in this part of Africa. This conflict is not new; it has a long and enduring history that is best grasped along the lines of *la longue durée*. However, it is also important to understand how this history takes new turns as it is influenced by other events, such as the imposition of the modern state system and the later economic alliance between the Mandingo and successive Liberian governments.

These events altered some aspects of the relationship between first-comers and latecomers, but the basics have remained strikingly similar. At the heart of the issue is 'citizenship', and therefore also the right to land. The belonging to the land is in essence what guarantees the rights of present generations as well as future generations. In places such as Lofa, protection of these rights is most effectively sought in tales of origin and storytelling about a collective 'we'. This 'we' is a unit – the nuclear family, the lineage, the community, the ethnic group or several ethnic groups – facing a perceived stranger, an other, an intruder, an enemy, somebody threatening certain rights seen as the heritage belonging to the 'sons of the soil'. In this kind of social drama, people such as Philip Kamara and Aliyu Sheriff are given a 'funeral for a friend' when they are put to rest by their kin. Other people saw them as criminal warlords, but the Mandingo of Bakiedou and Sakomedu read them as the current manifestation of the 'glorious' warrior tradition of the Mandingo, a tradition in which the soldier is both a keeper of the community and an expander of trade and other economic opportunities.

4 | KENYA: MAJIMBOISM, INDIGENOUS LAND CLAIMS AND ELECTORAL VIOLENCE

Violence erupted across Kenya in the wake of the 2007 general election. The violence took a number of commentators by surprise, undermining the assumptions many outside observers held about the stability of Kenya's multiparty democracy. In a matter of weeks, it was estimated that at the very least over 1,000 lives had been lost and over 500,000 people displaced. For others who had been following Kenyan politics for the last several years, if not decades, the violence was tragically unsurprising. Kenyan elections had increasingly been characterised by political violence, particularly after the return to multipartyism in the 1990s. In fact, the 1990s saw outbursts of political violence that were more destructive and at least three times more fatal than those the country witnessed in 2007–08. Like the politically inspired ethnic violence of the 1990s, the recent violence was the culmination of a number of factors and strategies. Central to the outbursts were discourses around autochthony and land claims, crystallised around the deployment of majimboism, understood by many to imply the forceful expulsion of non-indigenous peoples from the Rift Valley and the restoring of 'ancestral lands' to the 'native' Kalenjin and Maasai communities.[1] It would be a mistake to assume that the violence that occurred in the aftermath of the 2007 election was either inevitable or caused by the election. Like the other cases examined in this volume, the violence that erupted in Kenya was the product of a long sequence of historical choices, political actions, and decisions to activate certain narratives of identity and victimhood.

The 2007 election

The 2007 presidential election pitted incumbent President Mwai Kibaki, running under the Party of National Unity (PNU) banner, against former ally Raila Odinga of the Orange Democratic Movement (ODM) as well as Kalonzo Musyoka of ODM-Kenya (ODM-K). The competition was essentially between Kibaki and Odinga, who fought a bitter campaign, resulting in a race that many opinion polls considered too close to call. Those who did predict a winner, however, indicated that Odinga was likely to squeeze out a victory against the incumbent. Voting was held on 27 December and, according to official figures, the turnout was an impressive 70 per cent. As election results were reported slowly, it seemed that Odinga had a clear and unassailable lead. By Saturday, 29 December, Odinga was ahead by almost a million votes and the *Saturday Nation* was reporting: 'bar any *force majeure*, Mr Raila Odinga is poised to win the presidency and with parliamentary majority' (quoted in Lynch 2008: 562).

But election results from Kibaki's strongholds in the Central Province were the last to be reported, and they appeared to give the President a surge from behind that resulted in a win. On 30 December 2007, Samuel Kivuitu, chair of the Electoral Commission of Kenya (ECK), announced that Kibaki, with 4,584,721 votes, had narrowly defeated Odinga, who was credited with 4,352,993 votes. Odinga's ODM was quick to decry the results. In fact, even before the results were announced, they had charged Kibaki and the PNU with electoral fraud. Their claims were given significant legitimacy in the days following the announcement; the Kenya National Commission on Human Rights (KNCHR) and the Kenya Elections Domestic Observation Forum (KEDOF) held press conferences to air their concerns about voting irregularities (KEDOF 2007; KNCHR 2007). These concerns gained even more traction when the EU Election Observers Mission documented a number of gross violations. For example, in several constituencies the figures given to the EU observers were over 20,000 lower than the figures released by the ECK. The head of the EU observation team even claimed to have personally witnessed voting numbers changed in Kibaki's favour (EOM 2008).

In contrast to the close presidential vote, the ODM swept the parliamentary election (in what most election observers deemed were free and fair contests). Although they were unable to gain an outright majority in the parliament, the ODM won more than twice as many seats as the PNU. Moreover, a number of key PNU leaders and Kibaki allies were swept out of office. The discrepancy between the ODM's clear parliamentary victory and Odinga's close loss led many ODM supporters to assume that Kibaki had denied their candidate his rightful victory – although this assumption is strongly challenged by Nic Cheeseman (2008: 178–80), who illustrates how the discrepancy reflected voters' divided loyalties and interests.

It should be stressed that neither side engaged in a clean electoral campaign. There were substantial reports of vote inflation on both sides, in addition to voter intimidation. The reality is that the actual outcome of the vote will never be known. Kivuitu, chair of the ECK, publicly complained a few days after he announced the results that he did not know himself what the actual results were and that he was under pressure to release the results he had (*Daily Nation* 2008). This admission and his call for an international investigation further fuelled the belief that Kibaki and his regime had 'stolen' the election. Odinga and the ODM declared that they had no interest in going to court to contest the results, because, as they put it, they had no faith in the country's judicial system. The Kenyan democratic system, it seemed, had completely broken down. We are not interested here in uncovering the honest outcome of the elections, since it is clear that both sides engaged in electoral fraud. As Axel Harneit-Sievers and Ralph-Michael Peters (2008: 139) observe: 'While both sides rigged the elections, the government, using its administrative power, rigged more successfully and on a larger scale.' What is more important for us is the violence that surrounded the election and rose to enormous levels in its immediate aftermath.

Even before the election results had been announced, violence had swept across parts of the Rift Valley, as Kalenjin attacked and drove out Kikuyu. As we will discuss later, this violence was clearly premeditated. With the announcement of Kibaki's victory on 30 December, more intense violence erupted across Kenya, though it was mainly concentrated in the Rift Valley, Nyanza Province and Nairobi. By February 2008, it was estimated that well over 1,000 had been killed and at least 350,000 people evicted from their homes in the Rift Valley. The violence that erupted was not exclusively about the election, but was a convergence of multiple overlapping conflicts with different motivations and dynamics. While much of the violence assumed ethnic dimensions, pitting communities supporting Odinga (Kalenjin and the Luo) against those who had voted for Kibaki (Kikuyu, Embu and Meru), the underpinning discourse was about long-standing conflicts over land and historical grievances between autochthons/indigenous people and 'settlers'. Harneit-Sievers and Peters (ibid.) argue that the violence associated with the 2007 election can be seen as three distinct modes of conflict, each with its own internal logic and cleavages. The first was the political and social protest associated with the presumed defeat of the ODM, accompanied by violent attacks and heavy repression by the government's security forces. The second concerned a campaign of ethnic cleansing especially in the Rift Valley, which involved the mass displacement of 'settlers' and 'strangers' in an attempt by autochthons to correct 'historical wrongs'. The third is characterised as a more generalised form of ethnically informed violence, driven by armed militias. We will discuss all three at greater length below, but for now we want to note the vital role played in all three modes of violence by regional 'big men'. As we will see, regional big men were pivotal in activating autochthony discourses, ethnicising the political discourse during the campaign, and funding (if not directing) private militias and gangs that spearheaded the violence that engulfed Kenya. The political crisis did not come to a conclusion until UN Secretary-General Kofi Annan negotiated a power-sharing arrangement between Kibaki and Odinga, who was given the newly created post of prime minister, on 28 February 2008.

The 2007 election was a far cry from the 2002 election in which Kibaki succeeded in defeating outgoing President Daniel arap Moi's anointed successor Uhuru Kenyatta, thus ending Kenya African National Union's (KANU's) historic monopoly on power in Kenya. KANU had been in power since 1963, when Jomo Kenyatta led the country to independence after British colonialism. Kenyatta ruled until he died in office in 1978 and was succeeded by Moi. Under international and domestic pressure, Moi introduced a return to multiparty politics in 1991. But, through a range of machinations, he managed to win re-election in 1992 and 1997, before leaving the state house in 2002. Yet his hand-picked successor, Uhuru Kenyatta, son of the late president, was resoundingly defeated by Kibaki's National Alliance of Rainbow Coalition (NARC). Kibaki's stunning electoral victory had been brilliantly masterminded by Raila Odinga, who helped construct a multi-ethnic coalition to oust KANU. Within a few years, however, that coalition had fragmented and Odinga and Kibaki had become bitter enemies. This was partly caused by Kibaki's refusal to honour a Memorandum of Understanding in which he had pledged to share power with Odinga after his victory. Tensions were exacerbated by Kibaki's attempt to reform the Kenyan constitution in 2005. The proposed constitution, which critics claimed further entrenched power in the hands of the president, was defeated emphatically in a nationwide referendum, a defeat that was tied up with the land issue in the Rift Valley. Local Kalenjin politicians campaigned against the draft constitution on the grounds that the proposed national land commission would enable further land-grabbing by the Kikuyu in the Rift Valley (Lynch 2008: 559–60). Leading the opposition to the proposed constitution was Odinga and other former Kibaki allies. The icons used in the referendum – bananas symbolising a vote for the proposed constitution, oranges for the opposition – were appropriated after the referendum by the anti-Kikuyu forces as they attempted to forge a unified opposition, hence the Orange Democratic Movement (ODM).

Thus, in stark contrast to the 2002 election, when a multi-ethnic coalition drove KANU from power, the 2007 presidential election seemed to degenerate into a violent ethnic conflict. However, such a portrayal is misleading because it obscures the roots of the conflict. To understand the violence of 2007–08, we need to take a historical view of identity formation in Kenya, and particularly a view of how issues of land and autochthony claims have been activated across time and for different political agendas.

Land and identity in Kenya

Kenya is generally believed to have forty-two ethnic groups, with none in demographic dominance. These include the Kikuyu (18.3 per cent of the population, based on the 1999 census), the Luhya (14 per cent), the Kalenjin (12 per cent), the Luo (10.7 per cent) and the Kamba (10.2 per cent). Most Kenyans are migrants and have displaced others at some point in their history. Very few can claim to be autochthons – a word rarely used in Kenya, its synonym 'indigenous' being the preferred term. The people with perhaps the best claim to be indigenous were the region's hunter-gatherers that the British labelled 'Ndorobo' (also Ogiek or Okiek). The term is a corruption of the Maasai word for poor, and illustrates that the label was more of a contemptuous class demarcation than an ethnic distinction (Lonsdale 2008a).

Historian John Lonsdale has eloquently argued that the colonial creation of the Kenyan state also constructed rigid conceptions of ethnic identity tied to territory that did not exist in the pre-colonial era (Berman and Lonsdale 1992; Lonsdale 2008b). As he notes, before the British incursion, the area that became Kenya was a stateless space, decentralised and underpopulated. People's communal identity was shaped by their subsistence – farming, herding, or a mixture of the two – with loyalties constructed at the micro level of marriage alliances, age groups, trading partnerships and so forth. Conflicts existed, but so did co-operation and intermarriage, with the result being porous boundaries between communal groups. Moreover, as Elizabeth Watson (2010: 202) has argued, nature was understood as an open space, 'differentiated into known and named water and land resources and sacred sites'.

Colonialism represented a major disruption, as it did in the other cases examined in this book. With the advent of British colonialism in Kenya, nature started to be demarcated as 'territory', divided by international, regional and ethnic borders. Space became tamed, fixed and stabilised; an 'immobile closed system' (Massey 2005: 55) in which land was both a material resource and part of ethnic identities. As a consequence of colonialism in Kenya, ethnic identities became more salient, chauvinistic and based on territory (Watson 2010; Spear and Waller 1993). As Lonsdale (2008b) observes:

> What had previously been a multi-polar mosaic of scattered nodes of socially productive energy became, within Kenya's new borders, a layered pyramid of profit and power, unequally divided between two key centres – one 'white', one black – and many marginalised peripheries.

Central to this system was land. The colonial state gave white settlers 20 per cent of Kenya's fertile farmland, largely displacing peoples who would become identified as Kalenjin and Maasai.

At the same time, with the introduction of the concept of 'ethnic reserves' – in which territorial possession was legally delineated according to ethnic identity – land needed to be registered through a legal process, which worked to solidify the colonial idea of land privatisation (Médard 2008b: 384). The introduction of title deeds created new rules about land access and provided security of ownership, despite the considerable injustices that occurred through the expulsion and dispossession legitimised by this process. By the 1950s, these practices had spread to the African areas, and one can understand the employment of autochthony discourses partly as a rejection of the privileged position of title deeds, while at the same time firmly accepting the logic of land privatisation.

In order to increase state revenue, the colonial government

encouraged African farming on the remaining land. The primary African beneficiaries of colonial policies were the Kikuyu, who farmed on fertile land close to the capital of Nairobi, and were thus geographically well placed to enjoy some of the fruits of colonial rule, namely access to colonial schools, employment and European markets. As the various options for social mobility became increasingly tied to colonial policies and practices, British rule worked to promote an ethnic consciousness while simultaneously hardening ethnic divisions. Of course, those ethnic groupings were far from homogeneous. In fact, the emergence of Mau Mau can be understood as an intra-Kikuyu phenomenon in which poor and vulnerable Kikuyu joined the insurgents, while the propertied Kikuyu bourgeoisie, led by Jomo Kenyatta, engaged in more conservative and non-violent nationalist pursuits within the existing colonial system (Maloba 1998; Branch 2009).

Again, the connection between ethnic identity and territory was a colonial construction. As Claire Médard (2008b: 377) notes: 'In Kenya, the link made between land, territory, and ethnicity has nothing to do with ancestry and is, first and foremost, part of an administrative tradition.' The central component of this colonial policy in Kenya was the British scheme of land reserves. That is, the British introduced the idea that specific areas of territory were reserved for specific ethnic groups, with the 'White Highlands' preserved for European settlers. This institutionalised the practice of ethnic ownership of local resources, especially land. As Médard (ibid.) further observes:

> This heritage translated into the current administrative practice
> of assigning citizens to regions of origin, a fictitious affiliation to
> a large extent in a context of widespread migrations at a national
> scale.

Colonialism constructed rigid ethnic divisions and the claims of ethnic groups to 'traditional' land rights. Thus, in Kenya as elsewhere, the claim of territorial belonging – having innate rights to ancestral lands of origin – is a colonial creation that has become institutionalised and politicised first by the colonial state and then by the post-colonial neopatrimonial state.

As Kenya headed towards independence at the end of the 1950s, there were two important developments that are worth noting. The first involved the introduction of *majimbo*, a Swahili term that implies a sense of regionalism. It was introduced into Kenyan political discourse by European settlers in an attempt to retain control over the White Highlands through ethno-regional devolution. The idea was that post-independence Kenya would be divided into three autonomous regions, governed according to ethnicity, with whites controlling the Rift Valley, Kikuyu the Western Province, and the Luo the coast. The plan was rejected, but the concept of *majimbo* remained in the political imagination, implying both a sense of regional devolution and ethnically defined control over autochthonous homelands. This concept would be reintroduced in the 1990s and again during the 2007 general election, both times as discursive triggers for ethnically defined political violence.

The second development concerned a programme to transfer land from Europeans to Africans known as the Million-Acre Scheme. Land distribution schemes are central elements of the historical grievances articulated in relation to much Kenyan political violence, so a sustained discussion is warranted. The plan was implemented between 1962 and 1967 and aimed to settle Africans on 1.17 million acres of land in the former White Highlands. The original intention was for the settlement areas to be handed over to communities already living in adjacent areas, implying that these local communities would be reclaiming land that they were dispossessed from by colonial land-grabbing, or given to Africans who were already squatting on the land as tied labourers. Such a plan would have favoured those who identified themselves as Kalenjin, who were voicing traditional claims to the land as part of their ancestral heritage. The reality, however, was that the land was not given back freely, but was sold at prevailing market rates. While a few schemes were reserved for landless farmers, local communities were largely pushed aside in favour of market forces. By 1975, there were more than 250 settlement schemes across Kenya, with the majority in the Rift Valley. More than 1,300 farms had been purchased for settlement and nearly 70,000 families had relocated to these schemes (Abrams 1979; Leys 1975). These were a mixture of Kalenjin, Kikuyu,[2] and wealthy purchasers who often established large farms.

For local Kalenjin, the Million-Acre Scheme invoked a number of historic 'wrongs' that further contributed to a growing sense of melancholy, which, contradicting Freud, led not to paralysis but to deeply emotional levels of resentment. At the outset, the Kalenjin were upset that they were being required to purchase land that they felt legitimately belonged to them in the first place. Once the allocations began, many Kalenjin found themselves outbid by Kikuyu, Kisii and Luhya 'alien' buyers. Complaints about corruption in the allocation procedures increased and fuelled Kalenjin resentment (Lynch 2008). Later reports of Kikuyu going unpunished for failing to repay the loans used in buying the land became a further aspect of the Kalenjin list of grievances. In the 1970s, changes were made to the administrative procedure for the allocation of schemes, placing it under the direct control of the Office of the President. Thus, as Kikuyu continued to take up land in the Rift Valley schemes, blame was increasingly placed on the central government, especially Daniel arap Moi. As David Anderson and Emma Lochery (2008: 336–8) note, many Kalenjin came to believe that Moi had earlier acquiesced with regard to the influx of Kikuyu into the Rift Valley in order to become vice president under Kenyatta. Harneit-Sievers and Peters (2008: 134) claim that Kenyatta and Moi had struck a deal in the 1960s whereby the Kalenjin would redirect their own land interests to the north, leaving large shares around Nakuru and Laikipia for the Kikuyu, in exchange for the integration of the Kalenjin elite into senior positions within KANU. Many Kalenjin therefore maintain that not only did they fail to 'eat their fair share' under Moi (both as vice president and president), but they were actually victimised further (Lynch 2008: 550–2).

Land issues became more pronounced in the 1970s and 1980s as Kalenjin landlessness became more acute. Requests by local leaders for new schemes to meet Kalenjin population needs went unanswered. Despite this, the disputes about the land schemes remained non-violent and the Kalenjin remained relatively supportive of the KANU government. This changed in 2007, when the majority of Kalenjin defected from KANU and supported the ODM. This was due in large part to resentment of Moi for failing to enrich Kalenjin (beyond a few elite) and his attempt to create a family dynasty (ibid.: 545–52). This was also linked to the rise of William Ruto as the new Kalenjin 'spokesman' and his affiliation with the ODM. Ruto and other political leaders proved instrumental in the 1990s when they activated discourse about autochthony – or indigenous land rights. The reason for this is directly related to the reintroduction of multipartyism, elite fragmentation and spasms within the neopatrimonial system.

When violence around the 2007 election occurred in the Rift Valley Province, members of the Kalenjin community were the primary perpetrators, as they had been in the 1990s, engaging in attacks on 'non-indigenous aliens' such as Kikuyu 'settlers'. The Kalenjin label covers a number of subgroups that were administered as separate tribes during colonialism, namely the Nandi, Kipsigis, Tugen, Keiyo, Marakwet, Sabaot, Pokot, and Terik (ibid.). These groups form the majority of constituencies in the Rift Valley, which provides almost a quarter of the country's parliamentary seats. Because of this over-representation in the parliament, the Kalenjin have been a politically important group, one that voted as a near-united bloc in the multiparty elections of 1963 (supporting the Kenya African Democratic Union or KADU), 1992, 1997 and 2002 (supporting KANU). Yet Kalenjin unity was not an inherent fact, but rather something that had to be constructed. Much of that work was done in the colonial era, as the various subgroups were treated administratively as a unified grouping. Further attempts to solidify a Kalenjin identity occurred in recent years as a political strategy by local politicians to ensure representation and access to state power. Kalenjin politicians, such as William Ruto, have championed the need to create a greater sense of Kalenjin unity in order to increase their political relevance. Central to this project has been the incorporation of autochthony discourses centred on a narrative of historical grievance concerning land displacement in the colonial and post-colonial eras. As Gabrielle Lynch (ibid.: 554–5) has noted, the creation of the Emo Foundation (a Kalenjin Christian initiative), activities of the Kalenjin diaspora groups and the establishment in 2005 of Kass FM, a Kalenjin-language radio station, have been instrumental in constructing a unified and coherent Kalenjin identity. Contemporary Kalenjin identity therefore must be understood as part of a political project in which land, identity, autochthony and victimisation are central components.

Within this political narrative is a portrayal of the Kikuyu as arrogant 'guests' who were unwilling to 'integrate' with the 'host' Kalenjin community in the Rift Valley. Lonsdale (2008a) has pointed out that the tension between the Kalenjin and Kikuyu is not just about autochthony claims to who arrived on the land first, but also about debates over who has been more successful in 'civilising' the land. Just as the British had morally justified their colonial land-grab through claims of making the land productive, the Kikuyu regularly assert that they work harder than other Kenyans and have transformed the land through their superior labour, and justify their entitlement to the land because they have brought 'civilisation' and 'development' to the Rift Valley, in contrast to the lazier first-comers (ibid.: 309).

For the Kalenjin and Maasai, in addition to reproducing historical narratives of Kikuyu land-grabbing, the Kikuyu were regarded as being bad and ungrateful 'guests'. They were guilty of voting for politicians not supported by the Kalenjin majority and arrogantly giving Kikuyu names to local farms and trading centres. As Lynch (2008: 557) points out, in popular Kalenjin discourse, the Kikuyu-dominated Central Province 'was often described as the only "real *jimbo*", a place where few non-Kikuyu reside and no Kalenjin can do business'. Thus, as we see elsewhere in this book, autochthony claims were constructed upon historical narratives of victimisation of the autochthons by 'aliens', thus legitimising retributive violence.

The employment of *majimbo* in Kenyan political discourse

During his lengthy term in office, Jomo Kenyatta constructed an effective system of rule through multi-ethnic management and his savvy use of the neopatrimonial system. But the country Moi inherited in 1978 was substantially different. Perhaps paramount was the fact that there were fewer resources with which to maintain the neopatrimonial system of distribution. Kenyatta had benefited from being able to allocate land formerly held by the Europeans, but this option was far more limited for Moi (Lonsdale 2008b). Moreover, the economic recession further impinged on the resources available for the neopatrimonial state. To maintain his rule, Moi became increasingly reliant on a mix of corruption and repression. In the 1980s and 1990s, privileged individuals engaged in land-grabbing that became more blatant and corrupt. As Jacqueline Klopp (2000) has noted, this land-grabbing was not ethnically driven, but was related to greed on the part of the Kenyan political elite. In fact, this process resulted in political divisions among the Kalenjin, as some opted to oppose the Moi regime while others benefited from the regime's corruption (Anderson and Lochery 2008: 337). At the same time, the Moi regime engaged in the political instrumentalisation of ethnic divisions. This effectively obscured the class divisions that had become increasingly pronounced in Kenya.

Succumbing to domestic and international pressures, Moi agreed to the reintroduction of multiparty competition in 1991, in large part because he realised that it was the best strategy for his political preservation. One outcome of the restoration of multiparty politics was the fragmentation of parties according to ethnic groupings, as the ruling and opposition parties sought to mobilise the electorate by politicising ethnicity (Bratton and Kimenyi 2008).[3] With increasingly limited political resources set against a context of worsening economic conditions, Moi adopted a strategy of survival that included an exclusionary system of governance coupled with a policy of state informalisation driven by corruption and the looting of state resources (Branch and Cheeseman 2008). In particular, the Moi/KANU electoral campaign in 1992 was marked by violence and aggression towards its opponents.

In the Rift Valley, KANU exploited the land issue and ethnic divisions with brutal effectiveness. Ethnic communities who had felt marginalised under Moi (such as the Kikuyu and Luo) tended to join the opposition, while Moi's regime attempted to consolidate its power among the Kalenjin, Maasai, Samburu and Turkana. Proclaiming the Rift Valley a 'KANU zone', Moi and his regional allies engaged in a policy of political exclusion, targeting non-Kalenjin who were generally inclined to oppose KANU. It was during this time that Moi and his regional allies re-employed the term *majimbo*. In this context, *majimbo* was implicitly linked to a proposed policy of 'ethnic cleansing' in which 'aliens' and 'guests' would be driven out of the Rift Valley and their land reallocated to the autochthonous Kalenjin and Maasai. It needs to be stressed that this electoral policy was sanctioned by Moi himself and carried out by local KANU MPs, using state resources (Médard 2008b: 381–2). As Anderson and Lochery (2008: 337–8) observe:

> To carry out these acts in the central and northern Rift, local 'Kalenjin Warriors' were recruited into bands, and paid for their services. Those who participated in the evictions of non-Kalenjin settlers from schemes were often encouraged to seize the property and land of those who fled... As a consequence of this strategy, the local politicians who facilitated the recruitment and deployment of such gangs were rewarded and achieved enhanced status in their communities.

The employment of the *majimbo* discourse and the political instrumentalisation of ethnicity served Moi and KANU well, as they easily defeated a fractured opposition in the 1992 general election. They repeated this strategy again in the 1997 election, again with fatal effectiveness. During the 1990s, it is estimated that over 3,000 lives were lost and over a quarter of a million people displaced, mostly in the Rift Valley. Kikuyu and Kisii who had settled in districts claimed by Maasai were targeted for expulsion by Maasai leaders. The Kikuyu, the Luhya, the Kisii, and the Luo who had settled in land regarded as ancestral by the Kalenjin were likewise attacked and evicted through violence organised by Kalenjin leaders. In both cases, the administration was complicit in some of the violence (Médard 2008b: 382).

It is worth noting that throughout the 1990s political violence became normalised in Kenya, with the corollary being the rise of private militias and the decentralisation of violence. Moi and his allies (as well as his opponents) began to transform some of Kenya's gangs, largely made up of marginalised youths, into ethnic militias in an attempt to hold on to power through force. With elite patronage and funding, these gangs became increasingly violent. They also became regarded as vital elements for political success. Multipartyism and Moi's practices of governance through exclusion and elite rotation led to an increased fragmentation of the elite throughout the 1990s, which in turn fuelled the elevated role of political militias by the elite, who regarded Kenyan elections as 'high stakes' events (Branch and Cheeseman 2008: 4–10).

During the 1990s, the Moi regime was quite effective in its use of local militias. Employed during elections, they helped create an atmosphere of violence and fear that tended to deflate the opposition vote (ibid.: 13). Indeed, rival political leaders routinely employed gangs during election time, to the extent that groups such as the Baghdad Boys, the Taliban and Mungiki were engaged in proxy electoral wars. Perhaps the most obvious and successful employment of ethnic militias was witnessed in the Rift Valley during the 1992 and 1997 elections, as they became the militant personification of the majimboist discourse of 'ethnic cleansing'. It is important to note that these acts of violence took place not as part of the process of state collapse, but as a concerted political strategy conducted by a centralised state. Thus, during the 1990s, the employment of autochthony discourses and their link to political violence in Kenya were part of the state elite's strategy to maintain political control. The actual violence was often carried out by state representatives, with local police and district administrators deeply complicit in targeting the victims (Klopp 2000), as well as by marginalised Kalenjin youths (which we discuss at greater length below).

Again, it needs to be recognised that these militias were being deployed for political purposes under elite patronage. Because no single ethnic group has dominance, Kenyan politics has seen a growing reliance on regional big men, who mobilise their constituencies for electoral gain (see de Smedt 2009). As Cheeseman (2008: 172) argues:

> Many regional leaders, empowered through ties of ethnicity, lineage, and neopatrimonial networks maintained by their vast personal wealth, have proved able to mobilise vast communities, even in the absence of formal party structures.

While a number of these regional big men were complicit in the violent deployment of the autochthonous *majimbo* discourse, a few figures stand out, namely William Ruto and Henry Kosgey. Ruto was generally regarded as one of the primary architects of the *majimbo* campaign in the Rift Valley, and his colleague Kosgey was named in the subsequent judicial investigation as a key figure in inciting the ethnic clashes of the 1990s.

Unlike the elections of the 1990s, the 2002 election was hailed as a benchmark for elections throughout Africa and boosted Kenyans' confidence in their own democratic system. The polling was relatively free of political violence, in marked contrast to the two previous elections. A broad, multi-ethnic alliance led by Kibaki, but largely masterminded by Odinga (who even led the campaign while Kibaki recovered from a road accident), soundly defeated Uhuru Kenyatta, Moi's anointed successor. The victorious NARC had finally driven KANU out of power with promises to combat corruption and reform the constitution. However, the alliance quickly fragmented over implementation of the power-sharing Memorandum of Understanding and the question of constitutional review.

It should be noted that the 2002 election also marked the failure of Moi to cultivate a Kalenjin heir. His backing of Uhuru Kenyatta, a Kikuyu, angered many Kalenjin, who considered this yet another example of Moi collaborating in Kikuyu persecution of their community. Indeed, Moi's backing of Kenyatta exacerbated an intra-Kalenjin split between allies of the former president, largely Kalenjin elite who had benefited from the neopatrimonial system, and those who gravitated towards William Ruto. Rising to prominence during the 1990s, and implicated in autochthonous-informed majimboist violence, Ruto promoted himself as the new spokesman for the Kalenjin. In fact, on 3 June 2006, Ruto was crowned the foremost Kalenjin elder in front of about 50,000 supporters in Eldoret Stadium, with Kalenjin elders announcing that 'the leadership of the community had passed to a new hand' (quoted in Lynch 2008: 546). This was the second time such a ceremony had been held, the first being Moi's installation as the official Kalenjin spokesman in 1962. The marginalisation of Moi among the Kalenjin was confirmed by the 2007 election: not only was he unable to deliver the Kalenjin electorate for Kibaki's PNU, but every Moi-endorsed parliamentary candidate was defeated, including his three sons. To add to the ignominy, his own property was targeted and torched during the violence. In contrast, Ruto was brought into Odinga's ODM, where he became a key member of the party's 'Pentagon', a group of ethno-regional big men who were able to deploy their personal political machines to mobilise their constituencies.

Autochthony and violence in the 2007 general election

As already mentioned, the 2007 election was markedly different from the 2002 election. Most obviously, the former allies Kibaki and Odinga were running against each other, while former opponents Kibaki, Uhuru Kenyatta and Moi had become allies. The 2005 constitutional referendum had taken its toll on the NARC coalition. Kibaki was now running under the PNU banner and was reliant on a number of allied parties for support. The PNU was unable to maintain control over these allied parties; a number of them actually posted parliamentary candidates against each other and the PNU. In fact, the associated parties successfully demanded that the PNU provide funds for their own parliamentary candidates, resulting in a situation where the party spent more on rival parliamentary candidates than on its own (Cheeseman 2008: 174). On the other hand, Odinga was at the head of the ODM, which, in contrast to the PNU, was well organised and coherent. Key to the ODM's success was the existence of the so-called 'Pentagon', the main decision-making body of the party (made up of Odinga, Ruto, Musalia Mudavadi, Najib Balala, Joseph Nyagah and Charity Ngilu) that came to symbolise the ethno-regional nature of the ODM. Partly to reflect this patchwork quilt, the ODM devised a series of regional manifestos that were specifically tailored to address local concerns in each province.

In general, Odinga campaigned on a platform that included advocating a majimboist constitution. As the ODM tailor-made its appeal at the provincial level, the promotion of majimboism resonated differently with different populations. In some cases, it was interpreted merely as regional political devolution. People in the marginalised North Eastern Province largely supported ODM's promotion of majimboism because it seemed to promise a larger share of national resources than had been allocated in the past (Harneit-Sievers and Peters 2008: 136). But in other places, most notably in the Rift Valley, it was understood to imply the expulsion of non-indigenous people and the redistribution of 'stolen' lands among the rightful autochthonous communities of the Kalenjin and Maasai. Odinga, it should be noted, always kept his promotion of majimboism vague, never explicitly advocating expulsion. But for many in the Rift Valley, that was exactly how it was understood. Moreover, it is important to mention that Odinga's and the ODM's Rift Valley campaigns were led by key regional big men implicated in the 1990s *majimbo*-inspired violence, such as William Ruto and Henry Kosgey, as well as Kipkalia Kones, Franklin Bett, Zakayo Cheruiyot, William ole Ntimama and Sally Kosgei (Anderson and Lochery 2008: 330; de Smedt 2009). During the campaign, it was widely reported throughout the Rift Valley that a victory by Odinga would result in the expulsion of the non-indigenous 'settlers' and the restoration of land to the Kalenjin and Maasai. Kibaki's PNU employed the spectre of *majimbo* in their anti-ODM campaign, warning non-Kalenjin that they would be expelled if Odinga were victorious (even comparing Odinga with Idi Amin and Adolf Hitler in PNU electoral propaganda). In the weeks running up to the poll, hate leaflets and text messages were circulated widely in the Rift Valley, increasing the threat of autochthonous-inspired violence (Harneit-Sievers and Peters 2008: 136). Michelle Osborn (2008) has documented the importance of communication technologies, such as SMS text messaging, and their role in the violence by spreading fear and rumours among the populace. Rumours did not cause the violence, but they did shape public perceptions and informed people's actions. As Osborn (ibid.: 316) notes:

> Rumour can be shown to have stirred people to action, and in several instances there was a tangible connection between rumour and politics, rumour being used as a tool to reinforce a specific political agenda.

The level to which Odinga and the national ODM leadership were complicit in a campaign of violence is uncertain, but it is doubtful that they were involved to any great extent. However, it became clear after the election that such a campaign was premeditated. Both Human Rights Watch (HRW) and the International Crisis Group (ICG) have convincingly shown that local politicians and regional big men had established plans for a campaign against the 'aliens' immediately following the elections (ICG 2008: 3; HRW 2008: 37–8). Indeed, substantial political violence aimed at the 'non-indigenous' preceded the actual election. At least 380,000 Kenyans had been internally displaced by ethnically informed violence before the election and, by mid-December, some 10,000 people from Kuresoi alone had fled to neighbouring Molo (Anderson and Lochery 2008: 331). Almost 600 people were killed in the three months leading up to the election, and Cheeseman (2008: 170) has pointedly observed that the fact that 'this death toll received little comment speaks to the remarkable normalisation of violence within Kenyan political life'.

But there is substantial evidence that premeditated *majimbo*-inspired violence erupted in several places across the Rift Valley after the voting but before the results were announced, illustrating that violence was planned after the election regardless of the outcome of the vote. Within hours of the ECK's announcement, armed Kalenjin men arrived by lorry in multiple locations to carry out attacks. These attacks were not just aimed at 'non-indigenous' targets; they included attacks on Kalenjin associated with the PNU and KANU, and on properties owned by former President Moi and his sons. As Anderson and Lochery (2008: 333) document:

> The locations of this first major wave of violence in the first week of January show a clear spatial pattern: the outbreaks were invariably in places where non-indigenous populations were living. The targets of this violence were predominantly Kikuyu and Kisii communities, who were identified as PNU supporters. Though many attacks were murderous, the main purpose was to 'chase away' the victims.

One Kalenjin interviewed by the *Saturday Nation* proclaimed: 'Yes, we are unhappy about the election outcome. But more importantly, the presidential election result presented us with a good chance to "right" some of the historical wrongs committed against us as a community' (quoted in Lynch 2008: 567–8).

By and large, the police in the Rift Valley were unable, or unwilling, to contain the violence. Likewise, the local ODM leadership did little to rein in the perpetrators of the attacks. The government therefore sent the paramilitary General Service Unit (GSU) into a number of the hotspots (except for those in which premeditated barricades had already been erected to keep security forces out). Employing excessive force and intimidation, the GSU reportedly gunned down several dozen people in Odinga's ethnic heartland (Harneit-Sievers and Peters 2008: 139–40). Similar street battles erupted in the slums of Nairobi between youths and the security agencies. By mid-January, the violence became more diffused as other conflicts merged, but the ethnic character remained pronounced, with 'non-indigenous' labourers being targeted in the Kericho area and Kisii farmers in Sotik settlement schemes being attacked and their property seized.

As previously noted, the violence that occurred between December and February involved multiple conflicts and modes that all converged. In addition to the targeted violence against PNU supporters and their property, there was the organised autochthonous-informed majimboist violence perpetrated by some Kalenjin against 'non-indigenous aliens'. In the Nairobi slums, ethnic gangs battled each other and security forces, often engaging in attempts to 'cleanse' entire neighbourhoods that resulted in massive displacement and the grabbing of property. By late January, a wave of Kikuyu retaliatory violence erupted across the Rift Valley, led and organised by people associated with the Mungiki religious/political/criminal organisation.

The actions of the Mungiki and 'Kalenjin Warriors' in 2007–08 illustrate the growing role that private gangs and militias play in Kenyan politics. There is a political rationale behind the use of militias because they deflect culpability from their sponsors. When state security agencies engage in violence, the executive is clearly culpable. This is not the case when secretive militias employ violence. But, as Branch and Cheeseman (2008: 13) note, there are dangerous long-term consequences: 'Transferring the capacity for violence to ambiguous and complex structures necessarily decentralizes control over the use of force and reduces the ability of the centre to control conflict.' While the Moi regime might have been able to exert some control over the militias in the 1990s, by 2007–08 the informalisation of the state had rendered these groups increasingly autonomous. For Branch and Cheeseman (ibid.: 19), 'the decentralization of control of violence meant that the wave of attacks triggered by the declaration [of the election results] was broader and harder to manage than the government had envisioned'.

One of the more notorious groups employed was the highly feared Mungiki. The group began as a Kikuyu-based religious movement in the late 1980s but expanded its numbers and practices in the 1990s, becoming engaged in economic and political activities, most notably extortion and political violence. Despite being illegal for over a decade, and its political wing (the Kenya National Youth Alliance or KNYA) de-registered prior to the 2007 election, Mungiki is still highly active in Kenya's urban centres (Rasmussen 2010: 437). As Anderson and Lochery (2008: 339) point out, although Mungiki is depicted as an urban phenomenon, its origins lie on the farms and settlement schemes of the Rift Valley's Laikipia District, from which many of the early converts were driven by the majimboist violence of the 1990s. Significantly, discourses produced by Mungiki founders and followers stress a historic connection to the Mau Mau, particularly by articulating a narrative of victimisation by Kenyatta's land distribution deals (Rasmussen 2010: 444). Purportedly defending the poor and land-hungry Kikuyu and seeking 'revenge' for past wrongdoings, Mungiki is occasionally and understandably portrayed as the mirror image of the 'Kalenjin Warriors'. As Anderson and Lochery (2008: 339) argue:

> Both are ruthlessly exploited by a political elite that shows little will to enact the kind of land or constitutional reforms that might see the dispossessed and poor have their rights and entitlements protected under the Kenyan state. Thus, while elements of the Kalenjin elite fund the majimboists, those among the Kikuyu elite now collect funds to pay for Mungiki's 'protection' of the Kikuyu.

It seems fairly certain that the Mungiki retaliatory attacks were organised and financed by local politicians (Harneit-Sievers and Peters 2008: 141). The role of regional big men in the 2007–08 violence is well documented, as it was in the violence of the 1990s. HRW (2008: 37) reported:

> In the days prior to the election, local elders and ODM organisers in many communities around Eldoret called meetings where they declared that electoral victory for Kibaki would be the signal for

'war' against local Kikuyu. They told community members a PNU victory should be seen as conclusive proof of electoral fraud and that all Kikuyu were complicit in it.

Likewise, the KNCHR found evidence that some candidates had provided 'training' and funding to gangs of youths prior to the election, with instructions to target and expel certain communities (KNCHR 2007; ICG 2008). In the aftermath of the election results, many ODM leaders called on their supporters to 'go to the streets' in what many regarded as elite endorsement of violence. Prevalent among the rumours circulating in early January was that the government was about to 'unleash' Mungiki upon the Kalenjin. This rumour may have been used to justify 'pre-emptive' violence and certainly became a self-fulfilling prophecy by the end of the month. Jacqueline Klopp (2008) argues that one 'must realize that Kenya's violence today is fuelled by strongmen on both sides of the political divide. They are exploiting ethnic identity, pitting one community against another, as a means to gain power.'

Yet Lynch (2008: 566) asks why political elites engaged in such a strategy and why it resonated so deeply with some elements of the populace. It is certainly true that increasing numbers of Kenyan youth, in the rural areas but also in the towns, do not have access to land for cultivation. Yet, as we note throughout this book, constraints on access to land do not necessarily lead to violence. Indeed, there are other possible responses besides violence and autochthonous xenophobia. Her conclusion is that the autochthony discourse of *majimbo*:

> can be used by ordinary Kenyans to demand redistribution
> and bolster local claims to the ownership and control of 'ethnic
> territory'. The same individuals can then apply pressure on, and
> remove support for leaders, just as the latter realize they can gain
> easy mileage by supporting popular political positions.

In very simple terms, local politicians exploited historical land grievances for political purposes while many locals used the violent expression of majimboism to acquire land. Therefore the struggle is portrayed as collective, while the gains are individual (Médard 2008b: 382–3). As Anderson and Lochery (2008: 339) observe: 'Kenya's political elite has successfully turned the land question into an ethnic struggle over territory, thus avoiding the more obvious implications of a class struggle over property.' Of course, it is worth remembering that the Kalenjin were not united in their support of majimboism or its violent expression. As the evidence indicates, the primary perpetrators of the violence in the 1990s and in 2007–08 were marginalised young men who had the least to lose and much to gain.

The nervous language of autochthony: the case of Mount Elgon

Well before the 2007 election, the communities around Mount Elgon were experiencing horrific outbursts of autochthonous-tinged violence. Between September 2006 and January 2008, at least 600 people were killed and 50,000 displaced (Médard 2008a: 349). However, a closer look at this situation complicates how autochthony is used in Kenya and underscores a number of core arguments that we are making, most importantly the point that all claims to 'belong' are situational. As we have noted, employing autochthony claims is often part of an attempt to reify essentialist claims about identity and obscure the fact that identification is in fact a dynamic process. This becomes quite clear in the Mount Elgon case. But first, we need to recall that Kalenjin identity and its association with territory, which has been at the centre of autochthonous violence in Kenya for several decades, were administrative creations and not ancestral facts. Moreover, it is important to bear in mind that the 'Kalenjin' label was imposed colonially on a collection of subgroups who were administered separately. Indeed, 'Kalenjin' is an umbrella identity (like countless others across Africa and the globe) that can be divided into several sub-ethnicities, with those being subdivided further into smaller units. One may choose a given level of identification depending on the specific context.

Claire Médard (2008a; 2008b) has illustrated that, in some circumstances, these levels of identity become incompatible, such as in the case of the denunciation of Kalenjin identity by various subgroups living around Mount Elgon who are supposed to belong under its umbrella. Again, the purported trigger of identification and violent exclusion is territorial competition. While a Kalenjin unity is employed to legitimise autochthonous violence against Kikuyu and other 'aliens' in the Rift Valley, there are also separate demands for land among the subgroups. For example, the Pokot and the Marakwet in northern Marakwet District have recently fought over land, and the Nandi and the Keiyo in Uasin Gishu District have feuded over the repossession of former European land. But, perhaps, nowhere has this been more pronounced than in Mount Elgon, with the dramatic violence between those identifying themselves as Ndorobo (or Ogiek or Okiek) and the Bok. At the root of the conflict is the Ndorobo (Ogiek) claim that they are more indigenous than other Kalenjin in the region.

At the centre of this conflict is the Chebyuk area, which the state created in the midst of the forest reserve and turned into a farming settlement in the 1970s. The settlement, roughly 10 km² in size, was intended for the Sabaot, a subgroup of the Kalenjin. As Médard (2008a: 350) points out, the 'invention of the Kalenjin ethnonym came about ten years before the term Sabaot came into being in mid-1950s' (see also Lynch 2006). But by the 1980s and 1990s, a violent conflict had emerged as a dissident group identifying itself as Ogiek/Ndorobo began making autochthony claims to the land. As noted earlier, the label is used to denote hunter-gatherers, and is employed to evoke an indigenous claim to the land in contrast to the pastoralist settlers. In an illuminating development, during this time some Sabaot leaders were actively rejecting Moi's attempt to champion Kalenjin unity (stressing, in contrast, a unique and coherent Sabaot identity); simultaneously, others were rejecting claims of Sabaot unity as a façade for land-grabbing. The Ogiek/Ndorobo claimed that the 'Sabaot' label was being used to legitimise land allocation that victimised their own autochthony claims to ancestral territory. Tensions in the Mount Elgon settlement were exacerbated when the Moi regime enacted land reform in the 1980s that cancelled the initial land allocations, effectively destroying any sense of security in land ownership and instigating a process of land-grabbing in which the state was complicit. This heightened tensions between the Sabaot and 'alien' settlers, as well as within the Sabaot subgroup, as the Ogiek/Ndorobo increasingly articulated ancestral claims to 'their' land. The response to such dissent was the creation of the Sabaot Land Defence Force (SLDF), a militia group made up largely of people whose land was repossessed in the 1980s and 1990s. The SLDF sought to ensure a unified Sabaot identity and agenda, and engaged in violence against the Ogiek/Ndorobo dissident subgroup as well as against Bukusu 'invaders' (a subgroup of the Luhya) in the Chebyuk settlement and against the Kenyan state itself (Médard 2008a).

In some ways, the issues at stake in the Mount Elgon area are similar to the other conflicts across Kenya because they are rooted in soil, identity and history. They are exacerbated by demands for land and the crisis of the Kenyan neopatrimonial state. In Claire Médard's (2008a) excellent examination of the conflict, the discourses of autochthony and ethnic identity have become extremely complex in the Mount Elgon region as different levels of identification are activated in different contexts. It is useful to return to Stephen Jackson's (2006) observation that autochthony is inherently a 'nervous' language, because people who employ it always run the risk that their (ultimately unsupportable) claims of indigeneity can be undercut by others who claim to be 'more' indigenous. Such is the case in Mount Elgon, where claims to autochthony and communal unity at the level of the Kalenjin are undercut by the Sabaot subgroup's claims, which in turn are undercut by the Ogiek/Ndorobo claims of being more autochthonous and of having a more 'real' identity.

Future concerns

In August 2010, a new constitution was approved by national referendum. The constitution created more checks and oversight on presidential power, while also enacting the much-contested regional devolution of political power. Moreover, the new constitution created a land commission to settle disputes and investigate past abuses. The referendum was virtually free of violence, perhaps because both Kibaki and Odinga, as well as other key regional leaders, supported the new constitution. Whether this heralds a 'second republic' marked by the lessening of ethnic violence remains to be seen. But, as John Lonsdale (2008a: 310) observes, 'all Kenyans are well aware of the fragility of such fortune as they may possess, dependent as it is on the fickle trans-ethnic coalitions that determine whom the state will benefit and at whose expense'. It is doubtful that the new 2010 constitution will relieve those insecurities.

Almost as important as the new constitution was the January 2012 announcement by the International Criminal Court (ICC) that six Kenyan politicians – including William Ruto and Uhuru Kenyatta – were being charged with crimes relating to the 2007–08 violence. Three of these politicians (Kenyatta, Francis Muthaura and Hussein Ali) were supporters of Kibaki, while the other three (Ruto, Henry Kosgey and Joshua arap Sang of Kass FM) were supporters of Odinga. Interestingly, since 2007, Ruto has had a public break with Odinga and now finds himself closely allied with Kibaki. Whether this Kalenjin–Kikuyu connection will help heal the rift of the recent past is unclear, but it certainly illustrates the continuing reality of Kenyan political life, as elites fragment and alliances are constantly in flux. As has been noted many times, ethnic identification becomes rigid or flexible depending on the circumstances. And as Kenya heads towards the 2013 general election (in which Ruto and Kenyatta have both announced intentions of running), observers may be applauded for their optimism but excused for their cynicism. After all, there remains a very low level of interpersonal trust among political elites, and little faith in the ability of state institutions to enforce the 'rules of the game'.

Nic Cheeseman (2008: 168) remarked that, in addition to the violent explosion of politicised ethnicity, the 2007 election also revealed a number of social cleavages previously thought marginal to Kenyan politics. The first among these was the increased salience of religion as a mobilising issue. Likewise, age became an important predictor of voting behaviour. As Cheeseman notes, the 2007 election saw substantial generational change as younger challengers toppled a number of established dynasties, most notably the Moi family. But it remains to be seen whether the autochthonous-inspired political violence of 2007–08 marks the last desperate gasp of a political elite now driven from the political stage, with other social cleavages gaining greater traction among voters, or the beginning of a tradition of instrumentalising ethnicity on the part of a fragmented elite in a neopatrimonial system that seems to offer few options. The Kenyan case illustrates that ethnic identities become salient because they have come to embody other societal divisions, such as regional inequalities, control over land, and access to political opportunities. The instrumentalisation of ethnicity is often employed as a shortcut to electoral success while those larger social cleavages are ignored. In Kenya, political elites opted for xenophobic political mobilisation rather than denouncing corrupt political practices or addressing class-based inequalities.

Of course, land-grabbing has been a Kenyan political tradition for decades. The colonial regime engaged in massive land theft through a mixture of coercion and legal/administrative means. The post-colonial regime of Kenyatta likewise used state apparatuses to grab land and allocate it to allies within the neopatrimonial network. However, this became increasingly difficult for the Moi regime, as available land became scarcer. By the 1990s, Moi and his allies were exploiting ethnic divides to garner political support, and this also legitimised the use of individualised violence for grabbing land. Thus, the process of land-grabbing and reallocation had moved down from the state administrative level to the local level, organised and overseen by local leaders who utilised autochthony discourses to legitimise their actions, but still with state sanction.

Kenyans' desire for land is tied to the rise of capitalism and the view that land privatisation is a solution to all problems (Médard 2008b: 383). Within this is an inherent tension, as autochthony claims and the idea of the sanctity of private property seem contradictory. This tension has been exacerbated in Kenya by the state's willing failure to maintain a legal system to ensure the security of private property ownership. Given that, one can understand the employment of autochthony discourses partly as a rejection of the privileged position of title deeds, while still accepting the logic of land privatisation. As we noted earlier, the colonial regime introduced the concept of land registration to legitimise European control over fertile land. This process was extended unevenly to the rest of Kenya. In the 1980s and 1990s, the process of land registration sparked violence in many parts of Kenya, as the Moi regime treated land privatisation as a way to redefine land rights on an ethno-regional basis for its own political ends. Importantly, the Moi regime undercut the legal mechanisms that had existed to guarantee land ownership, arbitrarily applying and distorting rules for its own profit or political gain. Thus, title deeds and/or a history of occupation no longer provided security for those on the land. The 'rules of the game' had been undermined by the exact same state that was supposed to ensure that those rules were followed. In such a context, autochthony claims and violent expulsion and occupation became regarded as legitimate and attractive options for grabbing land. In some cases, the state plays a supporting role in activating those autochthony discourses, but as the Mount Elgon example illustrates, the state can also become a target of such violence.

5 | DEMOCRATIC REPUBLIC OF CONGO: 'DEAD CERTAINTY' IN NORTH KIVU

The Democratic Republic of Congo (DRC) has been a place of uncertainty ever since its current territory was carved out by Henry Morton Stanley for King Leopold of Belgium (see Dunn 2003), the consequences of which have been devastating. As René Lemarchand (2008: 30) rightly points out, no other place in Africa 'has experienced a more deadly combination of external aggression, foreign-linked factionalism, interstate violence, factional strife and ethnic rivalries'. Nowhere in this huge country is this more evident than in the eastern regions, and the province of North Kivu in particular. This is a place where certainty – or even security of identity and the politics of place – is of utmost importance as the alternative can have fatal consequences.

Many different attempts have been made to explain the conflict in the DRC. They range from ethnicity, to greed and resource wars, to the role of colonialism, and each and every one of them has made a contribution to the debate. However, while acknowledging this, we also argue that one advantage of an approach that places an emphasis on autochthony-based explanations is that they combine ideational and material elements through the direct link made between discourse/ narrative and access to resources. This may help us explain and give meaning to violent tactics that some of the other approaches fail to deal with adequately. Another advantage is that this approach helps us understand the local dimension of conflict (Bøås 2012a). Yes, of course the conflict in eastern DRC is connected to global markets and value chains through the extraction of coltan and other minerals, but its nature is local. There was conflict and lives were lost in this area prior to the major increase in the international demand for coltan. It is our view that way too much ink has been spilled on grand research designs that fail to incorporate the very local nature of most conflict on the African continent. This is very much the case in eastern DRC and North Kivu.

The crisis in North Kivu is often presented as an 'international conspiracy' and a 'resource war' merely about pillage and plunder (see Braeckman 2003; Collier 2007). The armed non-state groups of North Kivu are therefore mostly seen as collective actors who use violence to control the extraction and marketing of mineral resources. However, here, as elsewhere in Africa, the past and the present are connected in complicated ways. The conflict in North Kivu is by and large an agrarian war, and its root causes must be located in the complex web of uncertainties concerning citizenship and the land rights questions that have become an integral part of peoples' livelihoods (Bøås 2008). This situation is fuelled as well as further complicated by the extraction of the valuable minerals that are abundant in this part of the Congo.[1] This chapter will therefore display how armed non-state groups in eastern DRC, specifically in the North Kivu conflict zone, attempt to create order for their own operation, survival and navigation in a population from whom they seek support and upon whom they prey. Thus, we attempt to expose the ambiguous levels of attachment and disattachment that exist in this part of the Central African region be-tween armed non-state groups and their respective civilian populations. Although this chapter does not provide an exhaustive examination of the Congolese conflicts as a whole, it requires not only a brief summary of the larger war but also a discussion of Belgian colonialism and the effects of Mobutist rule to make sense of the current situation.

Belgian colonialism, the Mobutist state and the Congo War

The Congo is a European invention, created primarily through the work of two individuals: King Leopold II of Belgium and the explorer/journalist Henry Morton Stanley. Between 1874 and 1877, Stanley was the first white man to traverse Africa from the east coast to the west. During this trip, he charted the course of the Congo River and 'discovered' Lake Edward, Stanley Falls and Stanley Pool. Leopold II saw in this region a potential colony, something he had long craved. Under the guise of various international associations, Leopold II hired Stanley to acquire the land for himself (not, it is worth noting, for the Belgian state). During his 1879–84 expedition for Leopold II, Stanley demarcated the physical space of what became known as the 'Congo', extracting treaties (often through coercion) from local authorities that ceded their claim to land to Leopold II (Dunn 2003; Hugon 1993; Forbath 1977). Thus, the Congo was born, initially as the personal fiefdom of the Belgian king.

Prior to the colonial project, the area that became the Congo contained numerous and disparate ethnic, cultural and linguistic communities, including the Kingdom of the Kongo at the mouth of the river, and the Bolia states in the tropical forest, as well as the Lunda, Luba and Imbangala to name but a few. The diversity of the social, cultural, political and linguistic groups in the region that became known as the Congo has been documented best in Jan Vansina's *Kingdoms of the Savanna* (1966). As elsewhere in pre-colonial Africa, political space within the region is best conceived as a multilayered structure of concentric circles of diminishing control, radiating from the various cores (Kopytoff 1987: 29). African political and social boundaries in the region were rather fluid and shifting. Authority and power were dispersed into diverse and fluctuating forms of sociopolitical organisation: from states to non-centralised societies (Bohannan and Curtin 1995: 89). For example, before Stanley's arrival, the Kingdom of the Kongo – at one time one of the most centralised pre-colonial African states – had disintegrated into a fragmented, multilayered society devoid of any real chiefs. Moreover, the degree to which communal identities were connected to territory varied. As we will see later, in parts of the eastern Congo, access to land was often hierarchically organised, mainly around ruling versus dependent lineages. Yet, in one fell swoop, Stanley had physically delineated the Congo, established Leopold II's ownership over it, introduced or reified the concept of the political segmentation of territory, and established land ownership through legal titles. Furthermore, he invented the concept of a 'Congolese' identity, leaving Leopold II's colonial agents to impose it forcefully upon a highly diverse population.

The colonial state that Leopold II constructed was infamously violent and extractive. Joseph Conrad wrote his damning indictment 'Heart of Darkness' about Leopold II's Congolese venture, inadvertently saddling the country with the epithet that has haunted it ever since (Dunn 2003). The brutality of the colonial agents was remarkable and it has been reported that the population of the Congo was reduced by half during the years of Leopold II's rule, with a total of around 10 million fatalities (Hochschild 1998: 233; de St Moulin 1990: 303). The causes of death – other than 'natural causes' – included murder, starvation, exposure and disease, all of which had their immediate roots in the colonial project. Arguably, Leopold II and his agents differed from other European colonisers only by the degree of their brutality and exploitation, yet Leopold II's colonial project in the Congo became the target of international scorn. Images of colonial brutality, immortalised by the 'Red Rubber' campaign of the Congo Reform Movement, put tremendous pressure on Leopold II and he eventually relented and ceded the territory to the Belgian state (Hochschild 1998).

In the wake of Belgium's inheritance of the Congo from Leopold II, the colonial state instituted a colonial practice they termed 'paternalism' that portrayed the white man as 'father' and the African as 'child'; this became the philosophical framework of (and justification for) the Belgian occupation of the Congo (Hodgkin 1956). Stanley's colonising rhetoric continued to influence the colonial project, as evidenced by the Belgian colonial state's adoption of his former moniker, *Bula Matari* (breaker of rocks), for itself. As Crawford Young (1994: 1) observed:

> The metaphor captured well the crushing, relentless force of the
> emerging colonial state in Africa ... European administrators found
> this semiotic imagery congenial, as it suggested the irresistible
> hegemony deemed necessary to performance of their guardian role.

Through the simultaneous use of *Bula Matari* and paternalism, the colonial state tried to rhetorically construct itself as a 'tough father'. Its African 'children' would be 'raised' by discipline and control. Combined with the epic brutality of Leopold II's reign, the result was the establishment of a historical memory characterised by the legacy of state violence.

Shortly after Congo became independent on 30 June 1960, several units in the Congolese army mutinied, demanding promotions, pay rises and the removal of white officers. Belgian troops stationed in the Congo intervened and actively engaged the Congolese army and civilians. On 11 July, Moïse Tshombe, the regional leader of the southern province of Katanga, who had been denied a seat in the ruling coalition, announced his region's secession and successfully sought Belgian support. Tshombe framed the secession as a combination of ethnic nationalism and concern that the Congolese prime minister, Patrice Lumumba, was a communist. The breakaway region did not enjoy support from the whole of its population and the secession was largely driven by the desire to preserve Belgian economic interests and the region's comparative wealth. Although Patrice Lumumba and President Joseph Kasavubu succeeded in enlisting UN military assistance, the multinational force sent to the Congo did not move to dislodge Belgian troops from the Congo, nor did it initially engage with secessionist Katanga. In fact, Lumumba would eventually be captured by mutinous troops, flown to Katanga, where he was handed over to the secessionist forces, beaten, tortured and murdered. The Belgian soldiers initially provided direct support for Tshombe's breakaway government. Later, Belgian as well as French, Rhodesian and South African mercenaries constituted the backbone of Katanga's armed forces. These forces were able to repel UN forces until they were finally overcome in January 1963, with Katanga being reintegrated into the Congo (Gerard-Libois and Verhaegen 1961; O'Brien 1966).

The neighbouring province of South Kasai had also declared its independence shortly after Congolese independence, in part because of a deep rivalry between its leader, Albert Kalonji, and Lumumba, and in the wake of executions committed by Lumumba's troops in the region. It renamed itself the Great Mining State of South Kasai, with Kalonji proclaiming himself *mulopwe* (king of the Luba) (Hoskyns 1965). Lacking the level of foreign support that Katanga enjoyed, Kasai fell to the Congolese military at the end of 1961 after a brutal four-month war. Both secessionist provinces were driven largely by the political and economic interests of regional political elites, and, in the case of Katanga, their foreign business associates, who effectively employed the rhetoric of ethno-nationalism to garner popular support. Thus, it should be noted that recourse to ethnicity and autochthony by Congolese regional elites is not a recent development, but has its roots in the colonial and immediate post-colonial eras.

The image of stability in the Congo was more or less achieved after Joseph Mobutu seized power in 1965. Mobutu would remain in power for more than three decades. Ostensibly to help foster a common identity and replace the baggage of colonialism, he changed the name of the country to Zaire, as well as his own name to Mobutu Sese Seko. However, the country still experienced a number of secessionist movements (for example the 1977 and 1978 Shaba invasions) and armed uprisings throughout his reign. In general, Mobutu was able to stay in power through a combination of western patronage (which he deftly exploited during the Cold War) and an effective neopatrimonial system (Schatzberg 1991; Kelly 1993; Dunn 2003). Central to his domestic survival was the playing off and co-opting of his opposition, employing regional big men and, when necessary, politicising ethnicity. Indeed, despite his rhetoric of Zairian unity, Mobutu was quite savvy in his exploitation of political ethnicity for his own agenda. In general, the Mobutu years were marked by corruption, resource extraction and lack of development for the masses with the political elite enjoying considerable wealth.

After the end of the Cold War and with Mobutu's decreasing relevance to his western patrons, his Zairian state became more extractive and hollowed out from neopatrimonial practices. The country was in serious straits, its formal economy having shrunk more than 40 per cent between 1988 and 1995. Its foreign debt in 1997 was around $14 billion. At $117, its 1993 per capita gross domestic product was 65 per cent lower than its 1958 pre-independence level (Collins 1997: 592). It has been estimated that Mobutu and his close friends pillaged between $4 billion and $10 billion of the country's wealth, siphoning off up to 20 per cent of the government's operating budget, 30 per cent of its mineral export revenues, and 50 per cent of its capital budget (ibid.: 277–8). Physically, Mobutu's control effectively ended a few hundred kilometres outside of Kinshasa, while the rest of the country operated through a web of complex power relationships. Regional big men had always been at the heart of the political system, but they were largely obscured by Mobutu's and his international backers' employment of traditional discourses of state sovereignty. As these discourses underwent dramatic change in the 1990s and formal government structures withdrew and imploded, these regional forces were revealed in the full glare of publicity (see De Boeck 1996; Reno 1997; 1998; Turner 1997).

These tensions became apparent after President Mobutu's 1991 decision to hold a National Conference. One of the results of the National Conference was the exposure of the numerous tensions in Zairian society, not least of which were the tensions stemming from ethnicity and social identity, which Mobutu deftly exploited. Significantly for our conversations in this chapter, the representatives from North and South Kivu provinces in the eastern part of the country used the National Conference as a forum to attack the Kinyarwanda speakers in the regions, referred to as Banyarwanda and Banyamulenge respectively. The Kivu representatives sought to rescind the citizenship of these groups under the 1981 Zairian Nationality Act and force them to return to Rwanda and Burundi. As we note later, by 1993 armed groups began attacking Banyarwanda in North Kivu. Soon, the killings were in full swing, paralleling actions in neighbouring Rwanda. By mid-1994, thousands were dead in North Kivu and thousands more had sought refuge in Rwanda and South Kivu (Prunier 1997: 195).

On 6 April 1994, a plane carrying Rwandan President Habyarimana and Burundian President Ntaryamira was shot down over the Rwandan capital of Kigali. This provided the spark for several months of killing and fighting, now commonly referred to as the 1994 Rwandan genocide. The 100-day killing spree resulted in the murder of at least 800,000 Rwandans, the overthrow of the Rwandan government by Paul Kagame's Rwandan Patriotic Front (RPF), and the exodus of over 2 million Rwandans to refugee camps inside Zaire. These refugees were a mix of civilians, Interahamwe (the militia largely held responsible for the genocide) and members of the defeated Rwandan army (Forces Armées Rwandaises, FAR). The refugee camps quickly became controlled by the Interahamwe and FAR. Over the next two years, these groups (with the blessing of Mobutu's central government and, more importantly, regional strongmen) reorganised and rearmed. Soon, they began launching attacks from the camps into neighbouring Rwanda and against the Banyamulenge in South Kivu. After their requests for assistance were ignored by the international community, the Rwandan government and local Banyamulenge decided to take matters into their own hands by attacking their attackers.

The rebellion in eastern Zaire slowly began to take shape in August and September 1996, with the rebels launching a multi-pronged attack against the refugee camps, Interahamwe and Zairian army (Forces Armées Zaïroises, FAZ). Orchestrated and assisted by the RPF regime in Kigali, the rebels quickly moved from south to north, gaining control of the 300 miles of Zaire's eastern frontier and capturing the cities of Uvira on 24 October, Bukavu on 30 October, and Goma on 1 November. The refugee camps were attacked and disassembled. An enormous human wave moved westward, made up of refugees, Interahamwe and FAZ, all of whom were fleeing from the advancing rebels. Quite unexpectedly, thousands of refugees suddenly stopped and turned around. During the week of 10 to 17 November, the largest refugee repatriation in history occurred as the bulk of refugees walked back into Rwanda. By this time, the rebellion had acquired a name, Alliance des Forces Démocratiques pour la Libération du Congo/

Zaïre (AFDL), and a leader, Laurent-Désiré Kabila. Kabila was a former supporter of Lumumba and a member of the 1965 rebellion who had since survived as a small-time career rebel ensconced in the east and engaged in gold smuggling and the occasional armed attack (Cosma 1997). Kabila seems to have been plucked out of relative obscurity by the Ugandan and Rwandan regimes in order to give a Congolese face to the rebellion.

Kinshasa claimed that the rebellion was actually an irredentist manoeuvre by the Museveni government in Uganda and its protégé in Rwanda (see McNulty 1999: 53). Mobutu explicitly played the ethnicity card by portraying the conflict as one pitting 'Zairians' against 'Tutsi foreigners'. Employing autochthony discourses, he called for the 'citizens' to expel the 'alien' easterners from the country. As noted earlier, this reflected a long-standing utilisation of 'ethnicity' by the Mobutu regime to garner domestic power (Bustin 1999: 88). Throughout the 1990s, the Mobutu government had historically manipulated the ethnic tensions in the Great Lakes region, contributing to the outbreaks of violence and genocide. As the Bishop of Goma, Monsignor Faustin Ngabu, observed, 'the authorities, which should be coming to the aid of the victims of violence, seem on the contrary to wish to feed the flames' (quoted in Evans 1997: 45–6). In the dying years of Mobutu's regime, traditional and political leaders in North Kivu were encouraged to form armed militias, consolidating their power by land-grabbing and politicising ethnicity.

As the rebels moved westward, they were joined by other anti-Mobutists. Their external supporters included the regimes in Rwanda, Uganda and Burundi. Mobutu's counteroffensive collapsed as Kisangani fell to the rebels on 15 March. By April the rebels gained control of the mineral-rich provinces of Kasai and Shaba, thus robbing Mobutu and his power elite of a major economic lifeline. As the rebels moved towards Kinshasa, Angolan government troops poured across the border to assist them in the overthrow of Mobutu, who was being aided by the Angolan rebel group UNITA (União Nacional para a Independência Total de Angola). By 17 May 1997, Kinshasa had fallen and Mobutu and his entourage had fled. Soon afterwards, Kabila proclaimed himself the new president; renamed the country the Democratic Republic of the Congo (DRC); reintroduced the flag and the currency unit originally adopted at independence; banned political parties; and began to consolidate his power.

Within a year of Kabila's victory, his relationship with his regional allies, as well as with the international community, had soured. Various international organisations and foreign donors threatened to cut off aid and assistance because of Kabila's refusal to allow investigations into alleged human rights abuses – specifically the massacre of Rwandan refugees that had been carried out by his allies in the Rwandan army. More importantly, Kabila broke with his Rwandan and Ugandan mentors, and he demanded that they withdraw their troops immediately. Putting together another group of disenfranchised Congolese (some of whom had ties with or had been members of Mobutu's former regime), Rwanda and Uganda orchestrated another rebellion in eastern Congo – this time with the goal of deposing the man they had imposed a year earlier. The rebels included numerous unreformed Mobutists and disenfranchised Kabila supporters. By early August 1998, the rebels quickly swept through the east and, crossing the country in a captured aircraft, they moved into the west and threatened Kinshasa. In a desperate attempt to cling to power, Kabila convinced Zimbabwe, Namibia and Angola to shore up his regime by sending troops (Dunn 2002; Clark 2002). A stalemate ensued and, within a few months, the rebels in the eastern part of the country had splintered and eight neighbouring countries had been brought into the fray. Outright military victory was impossible, yet Kabila repeatedly thwarted attempts to realise a negotiated settlement, until a lone bodyguard assassinated him on 16 January 2001. Kabila's son and successor, Joseph Kabila, eventually signed a series of agreements that removed foreign troops and brought a tentative peace to much of the country (see Stearns 2011; Autesserre 2010; Bøås 2010; Prunier 2008). As part of the post-conflict settlement, presidential elections were held in 2006, with Kabila defeating Jean-Pierre Bemba in a run-off vote with 58 per cent.[2] The election did not immediately quell the violence in parts of the DRC and, as we discuss at length below, parts of eastern Congo continue to experience ongoing bursts of violence between various armed groups. By 2007, it was estimated that over 5.4 million people had died in the conflict (IRC 2007),[3] mostly from disease, starvation and other conflict-related causes, making it the deadliest war since World War II. It is within this larger context that we need to situate the autochthony violence that has plagued eastern DRC, specifically North Kivu, for years. The presence of what is currently the world's largest peacekeeping operation, the United Nations Organisation Stabilisation Mission in the Democratic Republic of Congo (MONUSCO), has not been able to stop the conflict.[4]

North Kivu – narratives of belonging and melancholy of the past

The province of North Kivu is located on the boundary between the more centralised kingdoms of Rwanda and Uganda and the more fluid political systems of Central Africa's forest regions. It is a place of mighty mountains, active volcanoes, dense forests, fertile soil, excellent grazing land and mineral riches, but also of immense population pressures (Vlassenroot and Huggins 2005). It is a meeting place and a melting pot, but also an area that has repeatedly tasted the bitter fruit of conflict, most often between groups claiming the status of autochthony and those defined as 'strangers' – migrants supposedly without the same level of attachment to a mythological native land (Bøås 2008).

Most of the migration has traditionally come from the east, and many Hutu and Tutsi had settled in North Kivu centuries prior to colonial rule. It is worth noting that the pre-colonial distinctions between Hutu and Tutsi were fairly blurred and porous prior to European intervention. As David Newbury (1998: 83) observes:

> The social identities we now associate with Rwanda [and eastern DRC] long preceded colonial rule, but they were not primordial; they have changed over time. In short there are histories of ethnicity, for not only has the nature of ethnic perception changed over time, but the different identities each has its own history ... Here as elsewhere, ethnic identities are not rigid, unchanging, or universal categories. But neither are they entirely ephemeral, fluid, and individual; they are socially-produced categories, not identities freely chosen.

However, under Belgian colonial rule, the division between the two groups became increasingly reified and politicised, especially after the colonial government issued ethnic identity cards in 1933. The Hutu–Tutsi delineation became further politicised with its entanglement in the colonially invented 'Hamitic hypothesis' (Sanders 1969; Malkki 1995: 68; Vansina 1990: 5). This theory postulates that the 'Bantu' (including groups such as Nande, Nyanga and Hutu) were the autochthonous inhabitants of Central Africa and that the 'Nilotes' (such as Tutsi and Hima) were historical invaders of the area. While there is no evidence to support such a claim, it has remained hugely popular in the region since its introduction by colonial anthropologists, and often underpins autochthony claims in the region – what Stephen Jackson (2006: 106–9) has called a 'megaethnicity'.

René Lemarchand (1998) has pointed out how, in addition to the Hamitic hypothesis, ethnically defined social memories have produced different historical myths and conceptual frameworks between the region's Hutu and Tutsi. The remembrance of genocides (past and future) has served as a formative element for social cognitive maps. Lemarchand writes (ibid.: 7):

> Genocide … leaves a profound imprint on the processes by which people write, or rewrite history, on what is being remembered and what is forgotten. What is being remembered by many Hutu is an apocalypse that has forever altered their perceptions of the Tutsi, now seen as the historical incarnation of evil.

In the wake of the 1994 Rwandan genocide, many Tutsi construct similar images of Hutu. Lemarchand also notes a tendency among many Tutsi (and we would suggest Hutu as well) to substitute collective guilt for individual responsibility (ibid.: 8).

Therefore, it needs to be recognised that the Hutu and Tutsi migrants into eastern Congo, regardless of when they migrated, carry these identity narratives with them. It should also be noted that the time of migration varies greatly. As mentioned earlier, some migrated into eastern DRC because of the 1990s violence in Rwanda, but many migrated from Rwanda during colonial times, i.e. after 1885. From the 1930s to the 1950s, the Belgian colonial governments transplanted tens of thousands of Rwandophones, both Hutu and Tutsi, from the neighbouring colonies of Rwanda and Burundi to territories in what is now the eastern DRC as part of a population control project (Willame 1997). Many others fled Rwanda after the 1959 Hutu revolution (Lemarchand 2008). These migrants are known broadly as Banyarwanda – in the simplest terms, the people who speak the language of Kinyarwanda. Through a series of migratory waves they now dwell in DRC as well as in Uganda and Tanzania. This migration took place through the centuries, and the length of residence and its history have shaped these communities. It is therefore not possible to talk about the Banyarwanda of North Kivu as a homogeneous group. It includes people of Hutu as well as of Tutsi origin, and even within each of these groups there are important distinctions. One example is the difference between the Banyarwanda Hutu living on the Bunagana hills on the eastern side of the Rutshuru highway and the Hutu living on the lower plains of the western axis of the road. The area on the eastern side has a much higher population density, and this has caused both more farming on marginal land and farms being divided into ever-smaller units. The consequence has been the creation of a landless population consisting of young men in particular. This trend is less obvious on the western axis. Thus, even within the same district, differences shaped by landscape, history and length of residence exist.

What these people have in common, however, is contested citizenship status and therefore also questions concerning their right to own land, to vote and to stand for election. According to the Congolese constitution of 1964, there exists only one Congolese nationality: 'it is granted, beginning from the date of 30 June 1960 to all persons having now, or at some point in the past, as one of their ancestors a member of a tribe or the part of a tribe established on the territory of Congo before the 18th of October 1908' (Jackson 2006: 104). Thus, the Banyarwanda could claim Congolese citizenship on the basis of ancestors being native to the DRC as of 18 October 1908. Those falling into this category could claim ancestral land along with other autochthonous groups in North Kivu. However, as the immigration and settlement of this group took place at different times and for various reasons, only a few qualified as undisputable citizens. This changed in 1972 when the Director of the Office of the President, Barthélémy Bisengimana, a Congolese Tutsi and Mobutu crony, masterminded a new citizenship law. The new law bestowed Congolese citizenship on all migrants living in the Congo prior to 1950. This gave a number of Banyarwanda political and economic rights that they had not enjoyed previously – suddenly they could vote, stand for election and, not least, buy land (Vlassenroot and Huggins 2005). In addition, this made it easier for them to organise, politically and economically, but also in the civic sphere.

However, this entire framework was changed again in 1981 when Anzuluni Bembe, another Mobutu strongman and an autochthonous Babembe from South Kivu, convinced the legislative council to re-open the nationality question. With a pen stroke, the 1972 law was repealed and a new law formulated that set the qualifying date back to the Berlin Conference (e.g. 1 August 1885). This had the effect of disqualifying almost all the Banyarwanda. Some undoubtedly had ancestors who had arrived in North Kivu as long ago as when this area constituted the western frontier of the powerful Nyiginya kingdom, founded sometime in the sixteenth century (Vansina 2004), but it was almost impossible to prove that this was the case (Turner 2007). The 1981 law was never implemented, but it still provided the institutional basis for increased discrimination against the Banyarwanda, and the issue resurfaced in the National Conference in 1991 – a national conference that the Banyarwanda had hoped would settle the citizen-ship issue. However, this was not to be the case as the delegations that represented their interests were refused admission to the entire conference on the grounds that they were not really Congolese citizens.

In North Kivu, tensions over political power and access to land exploded in anti-Banyarwanda violence in 1992–93 when armed groups of Nande, Hunde and Nyanga origin attacked Banyarwanda com-munities during what came to be known as the 'inter-ethnic war'. The refugee flows that followed the Rwanda genocide in 1994 further increased this tension as land became even scarcer, and the same was the case during the civil war that followed (Raeymaekers 2007). The consequence was that the importance of being able to confirm that one belonged to an area by ancestral connection to the land increased even further. The 2005 Congolese constitution was a step in the right direction as it dated ancestral connections to Congolese soil to the time of independence and not to 1885 or 1908. However, these shifting rules regarding citizenship have greatly contributed to insecurity among Banyarwanda. Importantly, the source of insecurity is the state itself; instead of being the guarantor of the 'rules of the game', the Congolese state has acted (and continues to act) in a predatory and arbitrary fashion.

As nationality is still tied to membership of a community dwelling on Congolese soil at the eve of independence, and since some of these communities also include people who arrived later, uncertainty remains. Moreover, manipulation of the citizenship question, which would undoubtedly lead to new conflict, is an ever-present fear. The results of a field survey carried out in 2006 illustrate this point as they showed that only people of Banyarwanda origin found it necessary to locate their right to land back more than one generation. This may seem strange, but the reason is obvious. For people of Hunde, Nande or Nyanga descent, this is not an important consideration as their tales of origin are not questioned. Nobody claims that they are not proper Congolese citizens. In contrast, despite the 2005 constitution, the people of Banyarwanda origin constantly have to argue their claim to Congolese citizenship and thereby to land (Bøås 2008). As targets of autochthonous violence, Banyarwanda are depicted as invaders, occupiers, aliens and strangers – allochthons par excellence. During the last few decades, it has not been uncommon to hear verbal attacks of these 'strangers' and calls for autochthons to chase them away. Political tracts abound in the region and warn of Rwandan (Hutu and Tutsi) expansion and machinations, and the need for the indigenous Congolese to physically drive them out (see Jackson 2006).

Non-state armed actors and land rights issues: epitaphs to a broken dream

As we noted, not all the Rwandan refugees fleeing into eastern DRC in the aftermath of the 1994 genocide were civilians. Among the refugee camps established by the United Nations High Commissioner for Refugees (UNHCR) were Hutu extremists from the Rwandan army and the Interahamwe. They blended with the civilian population and were in fact allowed to maintain their political and military organisation in the camps that were established. This eventually allowed them to control the camps. It was these groups that would later form the Democratic Forces for the Liberation of Rwanda (FDLR).

Both the first part of the Congolese civil war and its precursor started when ethnic Congolese Tutsi took up arms to protect themselves against government supporters and their allies among the Hutu rebels. Both wars started along the Rwandan border, particularly around Goma in North Kivu and Bukavu in South Kivu. However, the conflict rapidly spread along two main front lines: up the Congo River and along the eastern border, and to the south into the mineral-rich provinces of Katanga and Kasai (Mathieu and Tsongo 1998). In both wars, Rwanda and Uganda first denied participating, but later legitimised their interventions on defensive as well as humanitarian grounds.

What is clear, nonetheless, is that whereas Rwanda and Uganda may have entered the Congo with relatively clear motivations, such as pushing back the Hutu rebels and disarming the Ugandan rebels in the Allied Democratic Forces (ADF), these objectives quickly got tangled up in the complex conflict mosaic in eastern Congo. The regimes in Kampala and Kigali may have believed, and perhaps still do, that they were the ones calling the shots. This was not, however, how events were perceived on the ground. If we look at the situation today, it is increasingly clear that there is no easy answer to the 'who is pulling the strings?' question in these relationships. Rather, it seems like the Rwandan and Ugandan forces became involved in a series of local identity-based conflicts, in which they had little interest or knowledge.

The Rwandan troops supported the Tutsi groups that initially had taken up arms to protect themselves and their right to live in the area. First Kigali supported Laurent Kabila's AFDL and then, in the second phase of the war, the Rassemblement Congolais pour la Démocratie (RCD). Uganda, on the other hand, came to support Jean-Pierre Bemba's Movement for the Liberation of Congo (MLC) and various breakaway factions of the RCD, reflecting, at least in part, a Ugandan concern to facilitate the construction of an insurgency with a political organisation and not just a military campaign (Afoaku 2002). As the results of the 2006 elections show, Bemba did manage to build MLC into a political organisation as well as a military force, but not in eastern Congo. Campaigning under the slogan of *mwaka mboka* – a son of the soil – Bemba collected 42 per cent of the votes in the 29 October 2006 presidential run-off poll. He lost, but the election results also revealed a polarised country. Bemba did remarkably well in the Lingala-speaking western provinces. After losing the presidential election, Bemba won a seat in the senate in 2007. After the March 2007 violence in Kinshasa that pitted his bodyguards against Joseph Kabila's presidential guard, Bemba left the country, first to Portugal and later to Belgium, where he was arrested in May 2008 and transferred to the ICC in The Hague. He is indicted for war crimes and crimes against humanity, not in the war in the Congo but in neighbouring Central African Republic, where his fighters were invited in 2002 to help the then president Ange-Félix Patassé fight rebel groups.

However, during the conflict in eastern DRC, Bemba's MLC was just as much unwanted as the RCD. They were both seen as occupying forces, and this quickly spilled over into anti-Tutsi feelings among a broad spectrum of Congolese society that did not differentiate between the actions of the various armed groups of Tutsi (be they Congolese or Rwandan). This rapidly degenerated into a discourse tragically similar to the one that prevailed in Rwanda prior to the genocide. Once more the Tutsi were described as 'cockroaches' and the 'devil's children'. A political text circulating in eastern Congo in 2000, attributed to the 'Collective of Congolese Patriots', stated:

> History does not contradict us. The terrible atrocities committed shortly before the beginning of the 20th century by the Tutsi kings prove sufficiently to what extent you are descended from Cain. (quoted in Stearns 2011)

In North Kivu and elsewhere in the eastern provinces, the 1998 war against Kinshasa and the Kabila government by the RCD and its allies were countered by what was presented as a national resistance movement (for example the Mayi-Mayi). This placed the various Banyarwanda populations in a complicated position. They could seek the protection of the RCD, and some clearly did, but for the Hutu populations along the border this was difficult. The Rwandan regime viewed these communities with suspicion, as they believed that Hutu refugees who had been involved in the Rwandan genocide had infiltrated them. The result therefore was that many young men from these communities joined either the FDLR or one of the many Mayi-Mayi groups. None of these options could, however, provide long-term security guarantees for their home communities.

The FDLR is still considered a hard-core Hutu extremist group comprised almost entirely of ethnic Hutu fighters opposed to Tutsi rule and influence in the region. It was formed in 2000 as a merger between the Kivu-based Army for the Liberation of Rwanda (ALR) and other armed Hutu elements. Currently, it includes combatants as well as the family members of the combatants, refugees, and some political opponents of the Kagame regime in Rwanda who, due to the lack of other viable alternatives, have ended up with the FDLR. In popular reports, these different groups are almost exclusively presented as genocidal Interahamwe. However, this is true for only a minority of those who currently belong to the FDLR. The majority of them are men who came to North Kivu as refugees when they were young and have turned to violence both as a source of protection (fighting for the Hutu Banyarwanda) and as a means of survival. This suggests that the use of force serves a combination of livelihood purposes and strategies. In addition, as an increasing number of young Banyarwanda are forced out of farming due to a lack of land, forming a militia, or joining an existing one, also becomes an alternative survival strategy. Economic exclusion in the form of lack of access to land also inevitably leads to the erosion of traditional networks and safety nets. The end result has been the further marginalisation of rural youth. Deprived of the economic security that access to land gives, and having few other peaceful coping mechanisms available, many of these youths had few other life choices than the one that violence represented.

Thus, among the FDLR are people from the Interahamwe who took part in the Rwandan genocide in 1994, but also a considerable number of Hutu Banyarwanda who lived there prior to the genocide or are innocent refugees. Some are clearly of Congolese origin; others came as refugees and joined only after the movement had established itself in North Kivu. Many of the former had been forced from their land due to increasingly diminishing returns, as a combination of population pressure and elites gaining control over large areas for farming purposes led to a process in which smaller and smaller farms were established on more and more marginal land. This is particularly the case in the areas on the eastern side of the Rutshuru highway leading from Goma to Ishasa through Rutshuru.

The FDLR, therefore, has an external as well as an internal dimension and over the years it has become more integrated into the landless local Banyarwanda population. It fights against Tutsi groups and perceived Tutsi interests, but also preys on its own people as well as on Hunde, Nande and Nyanga communities (groups considered autochthonous to North Kivu). FDLR members have also married into and have partly taken over isolated Banyarwanda villages, from the Bunagana area on the Rwandan–Ugandan border north to Virunga National Park and the Ishasa border crossing and south towards Walikale. The FDLR has become attached to its local host communities, suggesting that it can no longer be considered an external invading group but is now an integral part of the conflict mosaic in North Kivu. Military action – as part of the agreement between Kinshasa and Kigali against the FDLR – not only fails to acknowledge this, but also sets in motion other local conflict dynamics that will have their own cross-border effects.

For their part, the Mayi-Mayi have at times been presented as a nationalist resistance movement, and at other times as a locally oriented youth militia without any kind of political superstructure or motive, or as different local ethnic militias acting independently of each other. In effect, the Mayi-Mayi combine all three dimensions. They draw on a nationalist rhetoric, often bordering on the xenophobic. They are youthful in orientation, discourse and membership. But they are also involved in land-grabbing operations on behalf of the ethnic communities to which they have attachments. This has been the case in both Rutshuru and Masisi. However, in order to understand both Mayi-Mayi operations and their slippery relationship with the FDLR, we must acknowledge both the degree to which the war and its divisions have discredited and destroyed most existing structures of authority and also the fact that these were not exactly solid prior to the war. The colonial project took little notice of the traditional organisation of African societies, and Mobutu's regime manipulated and reorganised traditional chiefdoms to secure loyalty and control (Mamdani 2001). In the dying years of Mobutu's rule, traditional and political leaders in North Kivu were encouraged to establish militias, consolidating their power through land-grabbing and ethnic wars (Pole Institute 2003).

Local resistance and the formation of militias are therefore not a new phenomenon in North Kivu. In this part of the Congo, there is a strong tradition of local resistance against any foreign control of the land. Often based on elements of traditional beliefs, local tribal militias have mobilised parts of the population in order to defend the 'traditional' order of control of the land. For example, as early as the period between 1900 and 1916, the Mwami of Kabare organised armed resistance against the Belgian colonial authorities based on Bashi militias, and in 1931 the Binji Binji sect, led by the prophet Ngwasi, had similar objectives (Njanga 1979). The name Mayi-Mayi also has several different historical origins. However, in its contemporary form, it appeared for the first time in the 1960s when local militias around Uvira in South Kivu allied themselves with the Muelist rebellion against Kinshasa. The name came into being as the combatants, in preparation for battle, chanted '*Mulele Mai Mulele Mai*', evoking the power of the *mulele*, the leader, to turn bullets into water. Thus, 'Mai' or 'Mayi' refers to the Swahili word for water and the ability of some to make 'water' that gives the warrior bullet-proof protection (Vlassenroot 2002; Mamdani 2001). Then as now, however, one important motivation behind the militia formation was to use the rebellion to their advantage in local land rights conflicts.

The current history of the Mayi-Mayi started in North Kivu, where from 1992 onwards marginalised rural youths, most of them without secure or permanent access to land, and dropouts from Mobutu's dysfunctional education system started to establish groups of youth combatants who perpetrated violence against the representations of modern political authority and the traditional authorities that they understood as completely corrupted by their clientelistic nature vis-à-vis the Mobutist state. Caught within a world where their aspirations for social progress and mobility were almost nil, these groups started to develop cosmologies about alternative social orders based on sentiments that can be described as a melancholy for a past that must have existed, but could not be articulated very clearly. Unfortunately, as some of the very first Mayi-Mayi groups were based in the central plains of Masisi and Walikale, they quickly became entangled in what was to become the 'inter-ethnic war' of North Kivu.

The 'inter-ethnic war' has become the name of a conflict that exploded when long-lasting tensions created by the 'nationality' question erupted in Walikale and quickly spread to both Masisi and Rutshuru. It started with the killing of a group of Banyarwanda (mostly Hutu) at the Ntoto market in Walikale by a group of autochthonous Hunde and Nyanga youths, but evolved into a civil war-like situation when the violence spread and Banyarwanda communities raised their own militias (Lemarchand 2008). By the time the violence burned out in 1993, more than 10,000 people had been killed and about 250,000 were displaced. The pretext for the conflict was a forthcoming local election and the advantage in politics, and thereby also in land rights disputes, the group that dominated those elections would gain. In short, it was an attempt by the autochthonous Hunde and Nyanga groups to dislocate the Banyarwanda from areas the farmers saw as their homeland prior to the elections. The reason for this was that leaders from the Hunde and Nyanga communities feared that Banyarwanda representatives would become too dominant due to their numerical strength, and that this would enable them to continue to keep land for cultivation for which they no longer paid tribute to Hunde and Nyanga chiefs. Following in the footsteps of the initial Mayi-Mayi groups, many more emerged during the Congo wars. Today, Mayi-Mayi has therefore become a generic term for all militias in the eastern parts of the country with some form of relationship to autochthonous authority and tradition.

However, even if the Mayi-Mayi as a social phenomenon is embedded in traditional practices and local historical contexts, their relationship with the traditional structures of authority is ambiguous at best. There is often intimate contact between the two, but traditional chiefs are not in total control of them – the formation of militias in North Kivu (as elsewhere) also offered young men the possibility of challenging age-based authority. It is in this process that we see not only how violence leads to a shift in influence to the advantage of those able to master it, but also the slippery relationship between the Mayi-Mayi and the FDLR. Several Mayi-Mayi leaders have formed ad hoc alliances with FDLR units, some based on calculations that 'the enemy of my enemy is my friend' – for example, they have a common objective to fight perceived Tutsi rule and imperialism. However, some of these relationships are constructed on shared experiences of enclave formation, as armed social units try to differentiate themselves from the social structures of their world by offering an alternative to the existing social and political order (or to the lack of such order). This seems particularly to be the case in the relationships developed between Mayi-Mayi and the FDLR units that operated in (or roamed around) remote areas such as the far corners of the Virunga National Park. Here, the relative isolation of these groups from other communities may have forced them into an initial cohabitation that was driven by practical pragmatism at first, but that later was cemented through shared narratives about neglect and precarious futures, and thereby a nostalgia for a past that seemed beyond redemption.

More than anything else, the FDLR and Mayi-Mayi have become an epitaph to a broken dream. The FDLR is currently not only one of the oldest armed groups in eastern Congo, but also one of the largest. Despite the fact that a good number of men have left, it is still a formidable fighting force. However, since 2004, it has not carried out any significant military attacks on Rwandan territory. Thus, as both a military and a political movement, it is lost in an unwelcoming borderland, but it still seeks to offer the hope of an alternative future through the construction of cosmologies about itself and, even more importantly, about 'paradise lost': Rwanda – the country that God had given them, the Hutu, as their birthright and that had been taken away from them by the offspring of Cain (the Tutsi). If it were not for the deadly consequences of the FDLR, there would be something immensely tragic about the whole situation. The

FDLR is a guerrilla force stranded in the rainforest and engaged in an eternal military campaign for the sake of the campaign itself – a rolling war without any prospect of movement – as its members train for an invasion, a triumphant return, that will probably never come. This is the irony but also the sadness of the apparent absence of purpose that the FDLR represents. Yet, it clearly does have a purpose, for it offers the promise of meaning and certainty as an antidote to the melancholic uncertainty of modern life. As in a shoal of small fish, the only safety is safety in numbers, so the ranks are closed and a strong Hutu narrative of past injustices and future redemption is reproduced. This refers back to a cosmology that draws on an extremist Hutu reading of the old Nyiginya kingdom – based on a potent but violent mixture of myth and religion. It is the old Nyiginya tale, not only of sanctuary in North Kivu but also of the aspiration of an eventual return home to power and prestige through violent means, combined with the narrative that if the RPF could survive five years in the bush, the enduring (and superior) Hutu of the FDLR can exist in this way for decades, even centuries if necessary. Rwanda is the land of the Hutu and one glorious morning God will allow his children to come home.

Even if the Mayi-Mayi lack the type of reason and reasoning of the FDLR, there are also striking similarities. Much of the Mayi-Mayi violence may seem meaningless, but it is not directionless. It is all about resistance, these days first and foremost against a Rwandophone conspiracy, and is thus a project for national resistance by the autochthonous populations against the Rwandans and their allies on Congolese soil. Embedded in the Mayi-Mayi project, or rather projects, is therefore a quest for a new order based on certainty. But this is a certainty that can be brought about only through a process of narrating memory, of constructing a tale of what can be remembered and what cannot be remembered. The melancholy of the Mayi-Mayi is the sense of being deprived of something, something that has been lost by the Congolese people. 'Why are the Congolese so poor, yet Congo so abundant in natural resources?' they ask. And in this question lies a nostalgia for a lost past, a past that can be brought back only if certainty about people and places can be re-established. This process of restoration has involved placing responsibility for the perceived loss firmly at the group level. In this narrative the culprits are the Tutsi, who are portrayed as 'alien' exploiters of Congo and the Congolese.

Laurent Nkunda and Rwandophones: protection and predation

After the RCD's poor performance in the 2006 election, the insecurity of Tutsi Banyarwanda remained high, especially as they remained targets of autochthonous violence from the FDLR, Mayi-Mayi and other armed militias. Because of this, General Laurent Nkunda's Congrès National pour la Défense du Peuple (CNDP) became an attractive option for providing security. Nkunda had fought with the RPF during the Rwandan genocide, with Laurent-Désiré Kabila's AFDL in the first Congo war, and with the RCD during the second. Offered a position in the new Congolese army (Forces Armées de la République Démocratique du Congo or FARDC) by the transitional government as part of the CPA of 2003, Nkunda and a number of other RCD officers chose to establish an armed militia. Nkunda claimed to be driven by a desire to protect his fellow Banyarwanda, but he was certainly also motivated by concerns that he would be tried by the ICC for allegedly orchestrating the killing of over 150 civilians in Kisangani in 2002. Supported by the Rwandan government, as well as by the provincial governor of North Kivu, Nkunda and Jules Mutebutsi led renegade soldiers on an attack on Bukavu in June 2004. Retreating to Masisi in North Kivu with other dissident Tutsi Congolese soldiers, Nkunda carved out an enclave and, in 2006, announced the formation of the CNDP with the purpose of overthrowing the government, although most of his military actions were focused on combating the FDLR and FARDC in the Kivus.

Drawing from Tutsi Banyarwanda as well as other ethnic groups who felt marginalised or at risk from attacks by the FDLR, Mayi-Mayi and Congolese army, the CNDP quickly became a serious military threat for the Kabila regime. In December 2006, Kabila attempted to broker a deal with Nkunda through his Rwandan patrons, with the goal of co-ordinating CNDP and FARDC activities against the FDLR (Vlassenroot and Raeymaekers 2009: 479). These operations not only failed to destroy the FDLR but resulted in the further displacement of thousands of civilians in North Kivu. Moreover, an anti-Tutsi coalition was established under the banner Patriotes Résistants Congolais (PARECO), comprising a number of Mayi-Mayi groups as well as Hutu CNDP deserters. Changing its tactics, Kinshasa decided to use military force against Nkunda rather than trying to co-opt him. The ensuing military operation against the CNDP, however, was a spectacular failure. The Kabila regime changed tactics again and decided to negotiate with the CNDP's patrons in Kigali. The result was an inclusive Conference on Peace, Security and Development in the Kivus in January 2008, bringing together representatives of different armed groups, civil society leaders and government officials. As Vlassenroot and Raeymaekers (ibid.: 480–1) note, these peace talks had the unintended consequence of increasing the number and size of armed groups:

> Given the advantages (including politico-military recognition and access to the demobilisation kits and other resources) of an official demobilisation, several armed groups increased their ranks. In South Kivu alone, since the Amani peace talks about 15 different militias could be observed, with an estimated total of 8,000 to 10,000 combatants. Some of these were remnants of former Mayi-Mayi militias, including officially integrated army units that started operating autonomously; yet other groups have been created more recently.

The peace talks had the ironic result of encouraging some inhabitants of the Kivus to return to arms because belonging to an armed militia improved their bargaining position and the possibility of political power denied through electoral competition.

Frustrated by events in eastern DRC and increasingly blaming Nkunda, Kinshasa renewed its military operations against the CNDP, apparently co-ordinating with the FDLR and PARECO – which, unsurprisingly, increased Tutsi Banyarwandan distrust of the Congolese state. However, the CNDP was again successful in repelling the attacks and, by October 2008, controlled large parts of Rutshuru and Masisi. After taking over the Rumangabo military camp, Nkunda's troops moved on Goma. It was clear that military victory over Nkunda was unlikely, as even MONUC forces had been unsuccessful in containing the CNDP. While clearly an effective military power, the CNDP's success was also due to three other factors. First was the support it received from the Rwandan government, including the military. Moreover, like other armed militias in the region, the CNDP also enjoyed support from a number of regional big men, not least the provincial governor. Thus, external patronage was extremely important for Nkunda and the CNDP.

Second, the CNDP was popular among many of the Banyarwanda in the region, not only because it offered an alternative to and protection from the FDLR, PARECO, Mayi-Mayi and other armed militias, but also as an alternative to the Congolese state, which was regarded as largely a coercive and predatory entity with little or no legitimacy in the region. This was certainly a continuation of the view held by many locals about the Belgian, Mobutist and now Kabila state. The third reason for the CNDP's success related to its effective extractive practices. Within the territory he controlled, Nkunda set up a parallel administrative structure. The CNDP controlled the police force, maintained its own intelligence service, and figures from September 2007 indicate that almost 1 million people paid different kinds of taxes to the CNDP and Nkunda (Spittaels and Hilgert 2008). The CNDP not only taxed the people who lived in the territory, but also collected taxes at several important junctions under its control. At these junctions the transport of minerals and timber, but also of other common goods, was taxed. One important roadblock for the CNDP was on the Goma–Walikale road at Mushaki; as much as US $10,000 in taxes may have been collected here weekly. Another important CNDP roadblock junction was in Kichanga on the road to Sake and Goma. This is an important route for the timber trade, and every truck loaded with timber had to pay about US $150 to pass through. Drivers were also frequently asked to 'donate' fuel to the CNDP at these junctions. The CNDP also indirectly controlled most of the petrol stations in Rutshuru and Masisi, whereas the charcoal market around Goma was evenly 'shared' between the CNDP, FDLR and Mayi-Mayi.[5]

The Tutsi are traditionally cattle herders and owners, and many of Nkunda's and the CNDP's powerful backers had important interests in cattle raising and trading. In particular, areas of Masisi have some excellent hilly grazing land and many large cattle farms are situated here. Meat is in demand in Goma, but also in Rwanda and Uganda. There is an intricate and complex regional market for cattle and meat that stretches all the way from eastern Congo to the Horn of Africa and into the countries in the Gulf of Aden and the Persian Gulf. In Rwanda and Uganda, dairy industries are quite well developed; one example is the plant located in Mbarara in Uganda, and others exist in Rwanda. In the latter country, cattle and what they produce (fresh milk included) are in high demand, but due to the population density not much grazing land is available. The solution found was that young cows of little value are herded across the border to Congo, where they graze in areas of Rutshuru and Masisi under CNDP control. When they reach sufficient size these cows are sold back to Rwanda for a good price. A full-grown cow is worth about US $600 in Rwanda. This phenomenon is known locally as *vaches sans frontières*, and even though estimates differ considerably, at least 50,000 head of cattle per year is not an unlikely number. The CNDP was quite effective in maximising its involvement in these financial exchanges.

Deciding that the best way to rid themselves of Nkunda was to deal with his Rwandan patrons, the Kabila government concluded an agreement with Kigali in November 2008. The agreement called for a joint military operation against the FDLR in exchange for Rwanda's removal of Nkunda. In January 2009, 4,000 Rwandan troops entered North Kivu, this time with Kinshasa's blessing. Signalling improved relations between the two countries, it also marked the first time Kigali trusted the Congolese state to deal with extremist Hutu in the region. While the joint military operation succeeded in destroying FDLR camps in North Kivu, the reality was that most FDLR merely relocated temporarily to South Kivu. Perhaps more significant was the replacement of Nkunda by CNDP Chief of Staff Bosco Ntaganda. The ousting was understood to have been orchestrated by Rwanda in exchange for the joint operations against the FDLR. Given his increased autonomy in North Kivu, Rwanda had decided that Nkunda was 'uncontrollable', eventually arresting him in late January. At the same time, it was announced that CNDP units would be integrated into the Congolese army, which prompted other groups, including PARECO and some Mayi-Mayi militias, to follow suit (see Vlassenroot and Raeymaekers 2009). While this has raised the hopes of many in the region, several armed groups still remain active in eastern DRC, a number of which justify their existence through autochthony claims. Central among them remains the FDLR, which continues to be active in early 2012. In fact, in December 2011, one of the FDLR's leaders, Callixte Mbarushimana, was freed by the ICC in The Hague after judges ruled that there was insufficient evidence to prosecute him. He had been charged with five counts of crimes against humanity and eight counts of war crimes, including charges of murder, torture, rape, inhumane acts and persecution, and destruction of property. This therefore suggests not only how difficult finding credible evidence in such circumstances may be, but also that the day when the FDLR comes to an end has not yet arrived.

Conclusion

The conflict in the Congo is to a certain degree like an onion (Stearns 2011), as it consists of layers upon layers and it is difficult to detect the core. Most likely, no single core exists, and therefore there is no single paradigm or theory that can explain the conflict. More than one approach is certainly needed, and, as much as we believe that ours offers important insights, we also understand the need to focus on the plunder of the DRC's natural resources and the external networks that support this illicit extraction and trade. However, we also believe that our analysis highlights the need for an approach that assumes that conflict always has a local angle and a local vantage point; in the case of the DRC and North Kivu, that angle is land, together with the questions about belonging that land rights conflicts give rise to.

We locate the melancholy of the Congo in the violence over land rights and in the sense of being deprived of something; within this sentiment lies a nostalgia for a lost past, a past that can be brought back only if certainty about people and places can be re-established. This 'certainty' is 'dead certainty' – the certainty of death – as it means firmly placing responsibility for the perceived loss at the group level. In this narrative the culprits are the Tutsi, who are portrayed as 'alien exploiters' of Congo and the Congolese.

6 | CÔTE D'IVOIRE: PRODUCTION AND THE POLITICS OF BELONGING

After some relatively peaceful years, the Mano River countries (Sierra Leone, Liberia, Guinea and Côte d'Ivoire) once more returned to international headlines when the 2010 elections in Côte d'Ivoire created a protracted crisis that was not resolved until President Laurent Gbagbo was captured in Abidjan on 11 April 2011. The turmoil started after the opposition candidate Alassane Ouattara, ex-prime minister (1990–93), clearly won the second round of the presidential elections held on 29 November 2010. Gbagbo, however, refused to step down, possibly hoping that eventually the Economic Community of West African States (ECOWAS), the African Union (AU), and the UN would consent and allow him to remain in a presidency that he had come to see as legitimately his. Eventually, he had to be removed from office by the force of arms and, in November 2011, extradited to the ICC, becoming the first head of state to be taken into the court's custody. The aftermath of this conflict will have repercussions and ramifications in the region at large, and particularly along the Liberian–Ivorian border.

In many ways, the ascension of Ouattara could mark the end of a bitter civil war – often regarded as two separate but connected wars – that was largely informed by the violent articulation of autochthony discourses. The first of these conflicts erupted on 19 September 2002 when an attempted *coup d'état* helped plunge the country into a bloody civil war. The war effectively tore the country apart, leaving the northern section controlled by a collection of 'rebels' and opposition parties under the banner of the G7. The G7 was composed of seven of the ten signatories of the Linas-Marcoussis peace accords of January 2003. Apart from the three rebel movements grouped together under the name Forces Nouvelles (New Forces or FN)[1] – the G7 included the two largest political parties – the Parti Démocratique de Côte d'Ivoire (PDCI) and the Rassemblement des Républicains (RDR), led by Ouattara, as well as the Union pour la Démocratie et la Paix en Côte d'Ivoire and the small Mouvement des Forces d'Avenir (MFA).

The government controlled the south. As Richard Banégas and Ruth Marshall-Fratani (2007: 82) observed, the Gbagbo regime maintained its power through 'a process of ultranationalist radicalisation via a vast apparatus of propaganda and parallel forms of control, surveillance and violence, most notably via informal militias and paramilitary forces'. After 2004, the two sides were separated by the UN-mandated multinational force ONUCI (Opération des Nations Unies en Côte d'Ivoire). The civil war ostensibly ended with the signing of a peace agreement on 4 March 2007. Central to the agreement was the holding of presidential elections, which were postponed several times. When Gbagbo refused to cede power, violence erupted again, in what some consider the 'second' civil war, although it is probably more accurate to regard it as a continuation of the first.

For decades, relations between northern migrants and autochthonous southerners had been tense, particularly in western Côte d'Ivoire where the majority of the country's cocoa is produced. As the Ivorian economy entered a state of crisis in the late 1980s, competition for land and cocoa revenue increased. This was fuelled by high rates of urban unemployment caused by the economic recession that sent many young men back to their villages in the south-west in search of rural economic opportunities. Here, the northern migrants became the scapegoats for the difficulties that the young men encountered when they returned to their places of origin. In the new Ivorian land law of 1998 they found the pretext to drive people considered migrants from the land. As early as 1999, more than 15,000 Burkinabé and Ivorians from the north left the south-west after bloody clashes around the town of Tabou, close to the Liberian border. When the Ivorian civil war started in this area in 2002, both the Ivorian government and the northern rebel groups recruited veteran fighters from the Liberian civil war. Between 1,500 and 2,000 Liberians fought for the Ivorian government and its support militias, whereas about 1,000 Liberians were enrolled in the ranks of the Ivorian rebel forces.

In the 2010 election that was supposed to bring the civil war to an end, Gbagbo received support from groups in the south and west of the country on the basis of an exclusionist populist rhetoric in which the groups who lived in the north of the country were portrayed as migrants or descendants of migrants who had settled the land at the expense of the original inhabitants. Naturally, the part of the Ivorian population that was the target of this rhetoric tended to support Ouattara, although there are exceptions to this rule. For many years prior to the November 2010 election, Ouattara was the country's leading opposition politician, but he had been refused the right to stand for election by previous electoral commissions based on the argument that he was not a full citizen as his parents were allegedly not born in Côte d'Ivoire but in Burkina Faso. The fact that Ouattara has identification papers showing his status as an Ivorian citizen was simply waved aside. The discrimination that Ouattara was exposed to reflects the autochthonous practices inflicted upon others.

What created the crisis in Côte d'Ivoire was conflict over basic political and economic rights: citizenship, land, voting rights and eligibility. What people disagree about in Côte d'Ivoire is the very basic question of who is entitled to which rights within the borders of the country. Who are full citizens and who are not? Who gets access to land? Who gets to vote, and where? Who gets to run in the elections? While this conflict destroyed Côte d'Ivoire's long-standing reputation for stability in a rather insecure region, the roots of the conflict go deep indeed. To understand the conflict – and the pronounced autochthonous character that it adopted – one needs to understand the lengthy history of labour migration, cocoa production and neopatrimonialism in the country.

A political economy of land, cocoa and labour[2]

As a multi-ethnic society, Côte d'Ivoire is comprised of about sixty ethnic groups, none of them in a position to dominate, at least demographically.[3] During the single-party period, the many groups that constitute the Ivorian polity were to all intents and purposes successfully balanced and co-opted by the post-colonial state. This success owed much to the astute political strategies of Félix Houphouët-Boigny, who became the country's first president after the French granted it independence in 1960. From 1960 to 1993, the country was firmly under his rule as he used the profits of the export crop economy to lock local elites to the state through his PDCI. This was effected in order to construct the widest possible elite consensus and was built on the distribution of spoils to various elites and on the marginalisation of those who refused to join in. Houphouët-Boigny also strengthened the colonial policy of intensive agricultural development through migration, which he encouraged throughout Côte d'Ivoire and from neighbouring countries in order to exploit the fertile southern region. This 'colonial compromise' (Mbembe 1992) depended above all on an institutionalised form of clientelism, oiled by revenues from cocoa. Beginning in the early 1980s, however, the foundation of this neopatrimonial system began to crumble under the effects of economic crisis, generational disputes for land and power, and the inability of Houphouët-Boigny's successors to maintain his delicate balance of power. The situation was worsened by the policies of liberalisation imposed on the country by the World Bank's structural adjustment programmes. The result was the collapse of the traditional social base supporting the regime – the Baoulé planters and the urban middle classes, principal beneficiaries of clientelist redistribution (see Banégas and Marshall-Fratani 2007). Yet, until the late 1980s, this system of inclusive patrimonialism worked remarkably well. The country was a haven of political and economic stability in an unruly region.

In this regard, the first thing we must recognise is the importance of cocoa. It was the first source of wealth in the country and still remains the most important one. It is the lifeblood of the economy, and both the economic miracle and the later recession that Côte d'Ivoire experienced are closely related to cocoa production. Côte d'Ivoire is the world's largest producer of cocoa: the country currently accounts for almost 40 per cent of global cocoa production. Fifty-six per cent of all cultivated land is used for cocoa production, and the cocoa sector may employ as many as 4 million of the country's 17 million inhabitants on what may be over 500,000 small farms.

Farming societies in the Ivorian cocoa belt emerged from historical processes of pre-colonial settlement, colonial conquest and peasantisation. Together, these factors worked against the concentration of power over people and land in the hands of indigenous authorities (Boone 2003). The south-east and central regions were settled over the course of the seventeenth and eighteenth centuries by Akan people fleeing from the domination and military might of Akan states in what is now Ghana (see Dian 1985). From these migratory movements arose the Baoulé and Agni ethnic groups of central and south-eastern Côte d'Ivoire. These migrants brought with them the kind of pyramidal (lineage-based) political hierarchies and kinship institutions associated with Ghana's coastal Akan monarchies and the Asante empire. However, the Baoulé and Agni institutions never developed a high degree of centralisation or wide geographical scope (Guyer 1970).

The rest of southern Côte d'Ivoire was home to a great diversity of localised polities without administrative centralisation above the village level. The sparsely populated west was the domain of widely dispersed societies that under colonialism were classified as the Dida, Bété and Gouro ethnic groups (Chappell 1989).

During the colonial period, the interests of France became centred almost exclusively on the production of tree crops, namely coffee and cocoa. The production of cocoa for export was initiated by the Europeans who brought the plant to Côte d'Ivoire. They were encouraged by the king of Anwi to create the first plantations around Aboisso in the 1880s. By around the turn of the century many of these had been abandoned and it was African planters who carried forward the momentum of cocoa in the region, while the geographical focus of European investment in plantations moved further west, outside Agni territory and into areas immediately to the north and west of Abidjan. By the 1930s, about 200 European-owned plantations were concentrated in the centre-west forest zone (mostly around Gagnoa and Oumé). These were huge by Ivorian standards, averaging 400 to 500 hectares, and were worked in large part by Africans recruited as forced labour by the colonial administration. However, these plantations were only marginally profitable and whatever prosperity they enjoyed turned out to be short-lived (Boone 2003). African smallholders, not the European planters, were responsible for the explosive growth of cocoa production in southern Côte d'Ivoire between 1920 and 1960.

The climatic conditions in some parts of Côte d'Ivoire are almost perfect for cocoa production. The cocoa tree is fragile: it depends upon a tropical climate with an average temperature between 24 and 28 degrees Celsius and an annual rainfall of no less than 1,600 millimetres, in an area where the soil is rich in organic material. The tree also needs shelter from the wind, and it grows best if shade can be provided. This is precisely the kind of conditions that we find in the tropical forest belt in southern Côte d'Ivoire. By and large, Ivorian cocoa is produced only in this area. This tropical forest zone is bounded in the north by an axis stretching from the Moyen-Comoé region (bordering Ghana) to the Montagnes region on the Liberian border, and in the south by the Atlantic Ocean (see Bøås and Huser 2006).

The contemporary political economy and the stratification of cocoa production in Côte d'Ivoire are the outcome of a double movement of transformation: labour migration from the north to the cocoa-producing areas of the south, in combination with a relocation of production from south-east to south-west. The geographic area in which cocoa production first took place in Côte d'Ivoire was the Région de l'Agnéby around Agboville and Adzopé. The very first cocoa plantation was established in Elima (close to Aboisso) in 1888 by the two French colonisers Arthur Verdier and Amédée Brétignière. The colonial production of cocoa involved local people, internal labour migrants from the northern and central regions of Côte d'Ivoire, and immigrants from Burkina Faso and Mali. Labour migration contributed directly to the imbalance between the northern part of the country, where about 22 per cent of the population lives on 53 per cent of the total territory of the country, and the southern part, where 78 per cent of the population lives on 47 per cent of the territory.

This demographic imbalance is neither a new development nor did it start with the introduction of cocoa. The tropical forest region along the coast has always been the centre of economic activity in this part of West Africa, and has historically attracted migrants from the Ivorian savannah zones and from neighbouring countries as well. However, this tendency increased when cocoa plantations were established, and the influx of migrants to the regions of the tropical forest zone seems to correspond to the expansion of cocoa production in this part of Côte d'Ivoire. The overall majority of Ivorian cocoa is produced on small traditional farms. According to a census carried out by Fafo for the World Cocoa Foundation in 2007, there exist nearly 500,000 such farms in the Ivorian forest belt. They are organised into different co-operative farmer organisations, from which formal and informal systems of credit are established. All of these farms practise diversification and co-planting as important coping strategies at the household level. This allows both for the mitigation of risk and also, equally importantly, for increased revenue and the possibility to spread revenue around the year as the harvesting season for cocoa is not the same as the one for other important agricultural products such as yams or cassava.

During the early twentieth century – after the introduction of cocoa – the social and economic relationship between migrants and those indigenous to the tropical forest zone was quite cordial. Land was abundant and everybody was able to carve out a relatively good living from their involvement in cocoa production. However, as pointed out by Ruf (2001), land ownership revolves around the cocoa cycle. In most cases, when a boom begins, migrants find land cheap and can acquire it easily.

> Most booms can be interpreted as situations where local ethnic groups, who control land, or at least have a moral claim to it, meet up with migrants, who initially bring and control labour. In this meeting, migrants are often the winners, at least initially, when labour is scarce. (ibid.: 293–4)

Some twenty to twenty-five years later, when replanting becomes necessary, land can become scarce, and if relocation of production is not possible, one may see increased conflicts between migrants and local ethnic groups. However, as long as relocation of production was possible, major conflict between migrants and those who controlled the land could be avoided.

When the rate of return on marginal land in the south-east became too low due to over-exploitation, many of the farmers relocated their production to the fertile, unused forest regions of the south-west. Therefore, even if most of the south-west became a cocoa-producing area later than the south-east, the area also came to experience labour migration from northern and central parts of Côte d'Ivoire and from Burkina Faso and Mali as well. This meant that the pattern of the south-east of the country was re-created in the south-west. In the latter area, however, the consequences were much more dramatic as this region has experienced the most intense conflicts over access to land and over land use rights. Today, the dynamic relocation of production has come to its last frontier. The process can no longer re-create itself, as there is almost no land left for pioneer farming. The integrative capacity of the forest belt is diminishing rapidly and it can no longer sustain the traditional labour migration from north to south.

In the central and western regions of Côte d'Ivoire, almost open land access and extreme labour mobility pushed the cocoa frontier westward, creating ethnically heterogeneous villages across most of the Ivorian south as hardwood forests were cleared to make room for small farms. Eventually, 'autochthonous–stranger' relationships similar to those we identified in the south-east were created across the entire forest zone. Malinke traders from Mali and northern Côte d'Ivoire (called Dyula) had already established themselves in the western forest zones, constructing towns and trade centres across the region. For the original inhabitants of this area, the newcomers were perceived as invaders just as much as the French had been (Person 1982).

After World War I, with logging and road building proceeding at a rapid pace in south-eastern Côte d'Ivoire, the Agni turned almost en masse to cocoa farming. However, as would be the case across virtually the entire forest zone, the limiting factor of production in the south-east in this period was labour. In order to expand their farmland beyond the limit of labour available within the household, the Agni of the south-east had to rely on migrant labour from the poorer parts of the colony, mostly from Baouléland and the northern half of Côte d'Ivoire. Thus, in the oldest cocoa-producing regions of Côte d'Ivoire, land pioneering and labour influxes drove the extensive form of cocoa cultivation, which became the defining characteristic of the Ivorian *économie de plantation*.

Already in the 1920s, migrant farmers had received access to forest land from the Dida, Bété and Gouro and had begun to invest in export crop production. Soon Baoulé farmers also began to arrive in the west. As this process evolved, groups claiming to be indigenous took up cocoa farming, clearing small plantations of their own. The Dida of the central west began to use non-kin labour to expand their cocoa holdings. First migrant workers were incorporated into households as 'adopted relatives', but outsiders also swiftly established land use rights, and less personalised relationships between 'indigenous' people and 'outsiders' became the norm (Chauveau and Dozon 1987).

The period from 1946 to 1960 was therefore marked by a huge influx of 'outsiders' into the central west region. By the mid-1950s this was perceived in many parts as a Baoulé invasion. Within a decade after independence, the Dida and Gouro had become ethnic minorities in their 'homeland' (see Zolberg 1964). It became common to find households transacting de facto land sales to Baoulé, Malinke and people from other parts of Côte d'Ivoire and beyond. Often these 'sales' were not acknowledged or respected by families and villages as such, creating a permanent environment of insecurity for immigrants and tensions in the relationship between the 'indigenous' people and 'outsiders' that became more intense over time. Thus, rather than being a post-colonial development, tensions between 'natives' and 'strangers' have been a prominent feature of Ivorian politics for decades, with the 1930s witnessing the foundation of the Association pour la Défense des Intérêts des Autochtones de Côte d'Ivoire (ADIACI).

From French colonialism to the state of Félix Houphouët-Boigny

The pattern of migration that developed was clearly based on economic incentives. However, it was also facilitated by the French forced labour regime. In general, the French regarded the northern half of Côte d'Ivoire and their entire colony of Upper Volta (now Burkina Faso) as a vast labour reserve. In 1932, the French authorities fused the colonies of Upper Volta and Côte d'Ivoire in order to perfect the forced labour regime. Redefining the colony's boundaries had the effect of doubling the supply of labour to the *économie de plantation*.

In Côte d'Ivoire, the nationalist era began in 1944, when African cocoa and coffee growers organised to protest against the colonial regime's discriminatory policies that favoured European plantation owners. It is also in this process that we find the background for Félix Houphouët-Boigny's rise to power. In 1945, he was elected as the Ivorian representative to the French Constituent Assembly. Houphouët-Boigny served for thirteen years in the shifting coalition cabinets of the Fourth French Republic, usually in the Ministry of Health. Here he forged an alliance with the French Communist Party for his campaign against forced labour in the French colonies in Africa. In a stunning victory for a deputy from Côte d'Ivoire, in March 1946 France abolished the forced labour regime in a law that bore Houphouët-Boigny's name. As a consequence, most Europeans abandoned or sold their cocoa farms. A direct result of the Loi Houphouët-Boigny was that those suddenly freed from forced labour could set up plantations themselves (Dian 1985). The outcome was decades of anarchic land rush in the forest zone. This has been described as a Baoulé colonisation of the Ivorian West (Chappell 1989; Nguessan-Zoukou 1990). Labour to fuel this post-war boom was supplied by migrants who came in their tens of thousands to the forest zone from the savannah regions of northern Côte d'Ivoire and from Upper Volta. In what became known as the policy of *mise en valeur*, the post-colonial government of Houphouët-Boigny granted land user rights to anyone who put unused land to use. At first this was unproblematic, but the spectre of all the unresolved questions of user rights versus lineage-based rights to land would later come back to haunt Côte d'Ivoire when land became scarce.

In promoting smallholder cocoa production, the regime of Houphouët-Boigny avoided the aggressively interventionist development strategies pursued by many of the neighbouring states. Producers' prices were set by the state, input prices were subsidised, and extension agents handed out cuttings for the planting of new cocoa trees. The post-colonial state did not build a heavy institutional apparatus or resort to intensive bureaucratic regulation to structure the labour process, investment, land access or the dissemination of new technologies. Even without much of an institutional apparatus to promote rural development, Côte d'Ivoire was able to triple its cocoa output between 1955 and 1970. This increase was almost entirely due to the replication of the smallholder production unit on an ever-widening geographical scale. The downside to this process was evident: low and stagnant yields, soil depletion and erosion, and low-quality output. The result was a permanent search for new land in the forest zone, which led to a constant relocation of production from east to west, and a continuous search for cheap labour. One corollary was the economic incentive to use child labour, as farms embarked on a search for cost control.

The regime of Houphouët-Boigny was clearly supported by rents extracted from the cocoa economy. The slush fund set up and controlled by the presidency during his time in office was connected to the cocoa marketing board and its associated structures (*filières*) and operated through a network of complex financial transactions. This established a sort of labyrinthine cocoa *filière*, an elaborate shell game with front companies, secret bank accounts, and transfers of funds with a multitude of layers of protection between the criminal acts and their beneficiaries. It has been estimated that for most of the period from 1960 to the 1980s, the peasant farmer was paid only about 25 per cent of the world market price for cocoa. About 10 to 12 per cent went to the commercial intermediaries, whereas the rest went to the *filière* system (see Boone 2003). This system was initially meant to benefit the Ivorian farmer through various schemes to support the price offered to farmers. However, more than US $100 million has disappeared from this system, some of it placed into 'accounts' in phantom banks and later used to buy weapons in deals managed by off-shore companies (see ICG 2004). Ivorians or people living there who have tried to investigate this system in more detail either have had to go into hiding or are currently missing. François Kouadio, an inspector in L'Inspection Générale d'État who undertook a study of the *filière* system in March 2002, literally had to run for his life, and is still in hiding somewhere in West Africa. The French-Canadian journalist and researcher Guy-André Kieffer disappeared on 16 April 2004 after having published a series of articles about corruption in the cocoa administrative system in *La Lettre du Continent*. It is widely believed that people in the cocoa sector with close ties to the then president Laurent Gbagbo were responsible for Kieffer's disappearance.[4] This should not come as a surprise as cocoa at that time remained one of the few economic foundations left at the Gbagbo regime's and its supporters' disposal.

Before the implementation of the *économie de plantation*, farming was based on rotating fields that were carved out of the forest, planted for one or two years, then left fallow for a long period (sometimes up to twenty years), while other fields were cleared and planted. In such a system, the farmer often experienced labour shortages, particularly during periods of sowing, weeding and harvesting. The limiting factor of production was labour, and the rich farmer was the one with many children and many clients, and most social systems in the area placed a high value on welcoming and incorporating 'strangers'. In this system, anyone not born in the village is a de facto stranger because land rights are shared within the lineage considered to be autochthonous to the village. Even if someone moved only a few kilometres away to another village, they would be required to find a host to sponsor them and arrange for their entry into their new local community. In the past, the mechanisms for incorporating a stranger were basically the same if the person in question moved just a few kilometres or if the distance were many thousands of kilometres. This has changed, and in no part of Côte d'Ivoire is this more evident than in the western regions of the country.

The politics of cocoa production and land rights, and therefore also the politics of autochthony in Côte d'Ivoire, are the outcome of a double transformation: labour migration from the north to the cocoa-producing areas of the south, combined with the relocation of production from the south-east to the south-west. The consequence is that land issues in southern Côte d'Ivoire are structured according to an autochthon–migrant dichotomy. The main point to take note of is that the smallholder cocoa plantation economy initially expanded in areas of low population density. In order to expand production, migrant workers were needed. These came from the northern parts of Côte d'Ivoire, but also from neighbouring Burkina Faso and Mali. They came as wage workers, but also looking for free land to create their own plantations.

The autochthon–migrant relationships that were established were similar to the 'stranger–father' relationships in Liberia and the forest region of Guinea (discussed in Chapter 3). In Côte d'Ivoire this structure is known as the *tutorat* institution. This institution establishes a bond of patronage between the autochthon and the migrant, to whom land rights are extended on the basis of the principles of a moral economy: any individual has a right to the amount of land necessary to ensure his and his family's subsistence. Autochthons therefore cannot deny land to a 'good stranger', i.e. one who accepts the duties given to him by the local community and thereby strengthens the community as well as respecting the prevailing socio-economic order. As an institution, the *tutorat* therefore regulates both the transfer of land rights and the incorporation of the migrant into the local community. The migrant, however, also owes the *tuteur* (the 'stranger-father') gratitude, which is expressed through gifts, labour and money. These gifts do not conclude an agreement on land rights, but rather perpetuate it – the agreement continues, being transferred to the heirs, and in principle is never-ending (Colin, Kouamé and Soro 2007).

Towards the end of the twentieth century, the integrative capacity of the forest belt had been rapidly diminished and was unable to sustain the traditional labour migration from north to south. In this situation, autochthons increasingly contested past land rights transfers under the *tutorat* institution in order to establish a new land fee or to get the land back. The economic recession in the country added fuel to this fire as many young men returned to the countryside from Abidjan and other major cities. On their return they often experienced the melancholic nostalgia that can make autochthony claims appear attractive. They noted that their old fathers were poor while those they perceived as strangers were rich. Returning educated youths have played a key role in encouraging their lineage to reclaim their land, and even demanding this (see McGovern 2011).

The melancholic nostalgia of *Ivoirité* and the 'Chocolate War'

The Ivorian 'miracle' had been based on cheap migrant labour and free access to land. When the economic downturn started in the late 1980s, the fight for diminishing resources became very bitter, and anti-migrant rhetoric among those who consider themselves 'true' Ivorians gained momentum (see ICG 2004). In the fiscal year

1989–90, the Ivorian government was forced to cut the producer price by half. Many farmers felt betrayed by the government, but their room for manoeuvring was very small. One of the few options they had available was to cut costs, and therefore employment of child labour was one possibility. Another was to increase the workload placed on children belonging to the household, either the farmer's own children or his 'adopted relatives'.

It was within this context of economic recession that Côte d'Ivoire was supposed to embark on a process of democratisation after the death of Houphouët-Boigny in 1993. The answer to the challenges that now emerged was the adoption of a policy of Ivorian nationalism. Under a slogan promoting '*l'Ivoirité*', Houphouët-Boigny's successor, Henri Konan Bédié, formulated a new electoral code, which in practice created two types of citizens: the 'pure-blooded' of Ivorian origin and those of mixed heritage. The idea was first and foremost to prohibit prominent figures in the opposition from contesting the elections by questioning their nationality (Nwokedi 1999). In this manner Bédié was able to engineer landslide victories in both the presidential and legislative elections on 22 October and 26 November 1995 respectively (Bratton and Posner 1999). The decision of the opposition parties – with the exception of the marginal labour party, the Parti Ivoirien des Travailleurs – to boycott the elections, the first in the post-Houphouët-Boigny era, was a serious blow to the legitimacy of Bédié's victory. This did not, however, prevent Bédié from employing a similar strategy in the 1999 elections. The concept of '*Ivoirité*' soon came to dominate the political landscape. As Banégas and Marshall-Fratani (2007: 85) note, 'the theme of "*Ivoirité*" rapidly came to be used as a powerful instrument of exclusion, at the service of every manoeuvre of stigmatisation and discrimination throughout the entire society'. Northerners were removed from posts in government and the army, and 'foreigners' were blamed for the economic crisis. They faced daily harassment and marginalisation as power was concentrated in the hands of a southern elite. This policy would later have devastating consequences in the cocoa-producing parts of western Côte d'Ivoire.

It was in this climate of discrimination and xenophobia that General Robert Guéï removed Bédié from power in a coup in December 1999. Initially Guéï tried to broaden his support base by including parts of the political opposition in his new government. However, Guéï soon returned to the same political discourse as his predecessor. In 2000, the government adopted a citizenship law that required both parents of a presidential candidate to be born within Côte d'Ivoire. This law was aimed at excluding Ouattara from competing in the October 2000 election. The election thus became a contest between Robert Guéï and Laurent Gbagbo of the Front Populaire Ivoirien (FPI). The election campaign was extremely violent, and for a while Guéï tried to prevent the votes being counted so that he could continue to stay in power. In the end, street protests forced him to resign and Gbagbo took over the presidency. Just like previous presidents, as soon as he was in power, Gbagbo started to manipulate the '*Ivoirité*' discourse. The only difference between Gbagbo and his predecessors was that the group now being promoted, particularly in the security forces, was Gbagbo's own group, the Bété (Hara and Ero 2002).

It is the totality of these events that provides the background for the civil war. In early 2002, the Gbagbo regime sought to exploit the citizenship issue and the division between communities by establishing a new identity card programme in which one's 'ancestral home' became the principal site for the production of identity and the basis of citizenship. Northern troops mutinied on 19 September 2002, demanding that citizenship laws be overturned. Co-ordinated attacks took place across the country, effectively dividing the Côte d'Ivoire between the rebel-held north and government-controlled south.

Despite the negotiated settlement to the conflict, the Gbagbo regime continued to propagate autochthony discourses that fragmented and segmented the Ivorian population. All 'immigrants' and 'northerners' were repeatedly portrayed as 'enemies of the state'. As Banégas and Marshall-Fratani (2007: 88) observe:

> In this context, semantic slippages are highly significant: since the outbreak of the war, the accent has been placed on 'patriotism', both by the government and the rebellion. This patriotism is measured by the defence of an imagined community which refers formally to the space of the national territory, but which has its historical foundations in the belonging to a localised space, leading to the progressive affirmation of a localised citizenship, rejecting local strangers to the margins of the nation.

In the government-controlled south, Gbagbo came to rely increasingly on armed militia groups called Jeunes Patriotes (Young Patriots), who actively propagated autochthony discourses and inflicted violence against 'strangers'. They did this in the name of a 'second war of liberation', justified by a melancholic story of loss and the exceptionalism of people and place, once more exposing the extent to which the mastering of such narratives propels actions and events.

In addition to the military – both the formal government army and the dissident soldiers of the FN in the north – the civil war witnessed a proliferation of armed militias. Even before the outbreak of civil war, Côte d'Ivoire had seen a rise in private militias tied to politicians and political aspirants. As Ruth Marshall-Fratani (2006: 31) observed:

> With the encouragement of local authorities and regional dignitaries with important positions in Abidjan, groups of 'young village patriots' have created a climate of terror in which strangers (northerners, Burkinabé, but also Baoulé) are chased off their land, which subsequently is seized 'legally' by local big men. In this process of expropriation, the youth use violence, but they also pose as defenders of a 'tradition' which they accuse their elders of having abandoned. Thus they reaffirm not only their autochthonous rights to land but also their growing ascendancy vis-à-vis the older generations.

Indeed, the role of the youth in stressing questions of national belonging, employing autochthony discourses and resorting to violence should not be underestimated, as we observe in other chapters in this book. The war in Côte d'Ivoire provided a formidable opportunity for the renegotiation of their status, and the employment of autochthony discourses was a significant feature in both legitimising violence but also challenging the existing social order.

During this time, the situation was chaotic in most of the country and particularly so in the western regions. This is the area where the double movement of north–south labour migration combined with east–west relocation of production met its final frontier, and became known by locals, as well as by international observers, as Côte d'Ivoire's Wild West (see ICG 2004). The tension in the cocoa-producing areas was extremely high between those who see themselves as autochthonous and those defined as strangers (e.g. migrants) with regard to the consequences of the policy of *mise en valeur*. Here, hundreds died in a cocoa feud – a 'Chocolate War'. The Bété people of the area, encouraged by the government and local strongmen, found in the civil war and the '*Ivoirité*' discourse a pretext to ethnically cleanse their neighbours and harvest their cocoa. The bumper harvest of 2003 fetched record prices and many got rich through the double harvest they were able to obtain. Some of the displaced cocoa farmers fled into internally displaced persons (IDP) camps in the area, but many more went into hiding either in the bush or in larger cities such as Abidjan, Adjamé and Trechville. A considerable number also fled over the border to Liberia and Guinea, or to the northern parts of the country controlled by the rebels. Interestingly, as destructive as the war was, it did not reduce Côte d'Ivoire's output of cocoa. In 2003, in the midst of the conflict, it still harvested 1.4 million of the world's total harvest of 3 million tonnes.

Elections and civil war redux

Land rights issues have been an integral element in the Ivorian crisis, and the post-Houphouët-Boigny era marks 'the return of autochthony in the guise of *Ivoirité*', as Colin, Kouamé and Soro (2007: 35) note. This was noticeable in the 1998 land law that used autochthony as the main source of legitimate entitlement, thus excluding not only foreigners from land ownership, but also Ivorian Baoulé and Dyula and other northern groups from legal land registration in the southern cocoa-producing regions. As the 'one-party state' descended into political instability and economic crisis, these tensions came to the fore as new rulers in the post-Houphouët-Boigny phase were asked by international donors to conduct simultaneous democratisation and economic liberalisation. This took place in a period of economic recession and immense political uncertainty, and the outcome was almost bound to be a disaster. The country was sent spiralling downwards into the pit of a war on 'who is who' – a war on citizenship.

Roughly speaking, the situation before the November 2010 elections could be summed up as a war between popular 'chiefs'. Laurent Gbagbo was carrying large parts of the south and in particular received strong support among the Bété population in his home area. Henri Konan Bédié of Houphouët-Boigny's old party had some support nationwide, but particularly in the middle belt among the Baoulé (Houphouët-Boigny himself was of Baoulé origin). Alassane Ouattara was the main candidate of the north and thereby of the country's Muslim population, but he also had a huge support base among northern migrants in Abidjan and among non-autochthon communities in the west. Guillaume Soro and the FN/Forces Républicaines de Côte d'Ivoire (FRCI) were the main armed group in the north, but also had an armed network in Abidjan (the so-called 'Invisible Commandos'). The last of the most important players were Charles Blé Guodé and the Jeunes Patriotes, with a large youthful following in Abidjan and other urban centres in the south and the west of the country.

As one election after another was postponed in the period between 2004 and 2010, it became increasingly clear that, if and when an election took place, it would be within an immensely competitive and conflictual patrimonial environment of exclusion. The most fatal heritage from the Houphouët-Boigny era was that none of the candidates who 'fought' to claim his throne could re-create his inclusive patrimonial social contract based on a *mise en valeur* approach to land rights. This had become impossible, and the only answer the politicians found was in a debate about '*Ivoirité*' – about who belonged and who did not. The outcome was a war on 'who is who' – who is a stranger, a non-autochthon; who should go home and who belongs and therefore has a right to land, to vote, to stand for election and so forth. In the end, Gbagbo was simply not ready to accept defeat, as the votes that mattered to him were the votes of the 'pure-blooded' Ivorians of the south. Ouattara and his supporters had waited for victory for such a long time that they would not accept a government of national unity after the model of Kenya (see Chapter 4). Thus, as Gbagbo lost the election, there was no other way out of the quagmire than a return to armed conflict.

In western Côte d'Ivoire there was fighting and inter-ethnic clashes between December 2010 and January 2011, in February, and at the end of March. Each of these periods of fighting created an exodus of refugees into Liberia. A much larger exodus was caused by the FRCI offensive that started in late March 2011 and ended in Abidjan on 12 April with the capture of Gbagbo. In just over two weeks the FRCI swept down from the north, assisted by the Dozo (a brotherhood of initiated traditional hunters), and broke through Gbagbo's defences.[5] This set in motion a series of revenge killings that caused numerous people to flee, not only the Guéré but also people belonging to groups not necessarily associated with Gbagbo. Around 250 people of Guéré origin were massacred – shot, killed with machetes and some even burned alive, and some dead bodies thrown into wells – at Duékoué after the FRCI had taken the town. However, in places such as Bloléquin and Guiglo, pro-Gbagbo forces carried out atrocities before withdrawing from these areas. In Bloléquin, forty people identified as migrants were killed by Liberian militias after they had separated them from a group of Guéré who were spared, and in Guiglo about sixty migrant workers from other West African countries were killed as Gbagbo's forces evacuated the area. Thus, particularly during the last part of the war, both parties committed human rights abuses in this area. The reason why the Guéré are afraid to return is not solely what happened during the war, but rather the combination of this knowledge with the realisation that they lost the war. Gbagbo is not going to return to liberate them and give back to them the privileges that they feel they have lost. Related to this is the question of who – if anyone – is in control of the western region and, in particular, the Guiglo–Toulepleu–Toe Town axis and the Guiglo–Man–Danané–Loguatuo axis. Who has replaced the old FPI/ Gbagbo parallel network that controlled the major parts of this area? Is the new state of Ouattara slowly regaining control and stabilising this area, or have alternative armed structures in the form of FRCI and their Dozo allies taken over? Most likely, the current scenario is a combination of these two things, and will remain so for the time being; however, as the situation in the western region and along these two axes in particular remains confused, there is little doubt about how the Ivorian refugees interpret conditions.

The situation that faces us is probably a protracted refugee crisis. In general, the non-autochthonous-claiming population feel that they were being 'liberated' when the FRCI and their Dozo allies gained control of the western regions in March/April 2011, and that they can now re-establish their farms (and expand them). On the other hand, the Guéré, as the reputed autochthonous population, and therefore collectively identified as Gbagbo supporters, fear reprisals and claim that if they return they are in danger of being killed by armed men blocking their safe passage to their homes of origin and their farms. This is quite telling as it illustrates the very agrarian nature of the conflict in Côte d'Ivoire and particularly in the western regions. Here, land conflicts have become increasingly militarised and tense through a vicious circle of war, displacement and return that has been going on ever since the beginning of this millennium. If and when the

Guéré start to return from Liberia in large numbers, there is every likelihood that the land disputes will multiply once more.

Conclusion

Supporters of Gbagbo claimed to be fighting a 'second war of liberation' on behalf of the autochthonous-claiming populations in the western regions. This rhetoric was and continues to be popular among many Bété, Guéré and We farmers, and it is on the basis of the meta-narratives that feed this rhetoric that Gbagbo's supporters built and organised their power structures. The result was an exclusionist and violent form of nationalism, without much potential for peaceful reconciliation or the development of an autonomous civil society. The November 2010 elections produced an eventual winner, but certainly not national reconciliation. The resentment and bitterness among Gbagbo's supporters run deep, and will most likely be exacerbated by the transfer of Gbagbo to ICC custody in The Hague, where he faces charges of being 'an indirect co-perpetrator' of murder, rape, persecution and other inhumane acts (i.e. crimes against humanity) that reportedly took place between 16 December 2010 and 12 April 2011. International human rights groups welcomed his arrest, but other observers were more cautious, warning against 'justice of the victorious'. In Côte d'Ivoire, the news about Gbagbo's transfer to The Hague was received as quite a shock. Even if Ouattara had been steadfast in his promise to hand Gbagbo over to the ICC, many of Gbagbo's supporters had hoped for a compromise as a bid for national reconciliation, especially before the 11 December legislative elections. After all, they assumed, Côte d'Ivoire is not one of the member countries covered by the ICC. Thus, to some, such as Toussaint Alain, former senior adviser to Gbagbo, this was a 'political manoeuvre designed to liquidate President Gbagbo' (BBC, 30 November 2011). In Abidjan, the front cover of 30 November's *Notre Voie*, the newspaper of Gbagbo's FPI, proclaimed 'Adieu la reconciliation!' ICC's chief prosecutor Luis Moreno-Ocampo tried to fend off such criticism by issuing a statement saying that 'Gbagbo is the first to be brought to account, there is more to come' (ICC, 30 November 2011). This rhetoric may work, but only if senior individuals on the Ouattara side are also brought to The Hague, as the country was almost as divided during the 2010 elections as it was during the civil war.

Quite predictably, Gbagbo's party, the FPI, pulled out of the

11 December parliamentary elections in protest, accusing the electoral commission of bias in favour of Ouattara, and the army of intimidating opposition supporters during the campaign. Ironically, this is almost exactly the same accusation that Ouattara and his supporters put forward when they were in opposition. In the end, the elections passed off peacefully, even in pro-Gbagbo areas of the country, but voter turnout was low. The question remains whether this was a direct effect of the FPI boycott – at the least it created a situation where almost all candidates belonged to the pro-government coalition – or whether it was simply a result of few bothering to vote as the national assembly has very limited powers. Whatever the case may be, it means not only that the conflict has gone full circle, with the pro-Gbagbo opposition using the same arguments that Ouattara made when he was in opposition, but also that the new Ouattara government is starting with a weak mandate. What this means for the government's willingness and ability to confront the poisonous cocktail that the nexus of land rights and citizenship has become in Côte d'Ivoire is a question that remains to be answered.

7 | CONCLUSION

Autochthony is a strategy, not a fact. But, at the same time, it is much more than just a rational-choice political strategy. The four empirical case studies have illustrated this quite powerfully. In objective terms, the groups claiming to be autochthonous in each case are more a consequence of state-building practices than historically coherent groups with a common distant past. Be that as it may, what is important for our purpose is not what is historically correct (if anybody actually can tell), but the meta-narratives based on which current groups in conflict imagine their collective memory. These cases illustrate the emotional intensity tied up in such autochthony claims. The potential explosiveness of emotions inspired by this discourse should not be underestimated. Clearly, the articulators of autochthony rhetoric are aware of its emotional impact, given that that is the primary reason for its ability to mobilise. But, as the four cases illustrate, once these ideas of belonging catch fire, the strong emotions unleashed can often overtake the leaders and their strategic agenda. Thus, the melancholy of autochthony does not always lead to a paralysis à la Freud, but may also inspire feverish activity and violence.

While these cases show how unstable and violent manifestations of the autochthony strategy can be, they also illustrate how politically lucrative this strategy can be – for both the regional big men fanning the flames of autochthonous rhetoric and the young men seizing land from their neighbouring 'strangers'. The cases of Côte d'Ivoire, DRC, Kenya and Liberia all illustrate the political rationality that makes autochthony an attractive option for political leaders in their attempts either to increase their power or to hold on to it. And for local populations trying to come to grips with their increasingly difficult daily lives, the autochthony discourse offers a politics of memory that makes it possible to construct an understanding of one's trying circumstances. These narratives of the past provide the comfort that life does not have to – and should not – be like this. Thus, the emotional resonance of autochthony narratives produces a spectre of melancholy while its explosive potential provides an escape from paralysis. Faced with a melancholic nostalgia for a lost past, autochthony can provide a strategy for redemption by identifying those who are responsible for this predicament, coupled with a call for their forceful eviction.

Yet why do we see such extremely violent expressions of autochthony playing a central role in these four cases, but not in other parts of Africa where people are also facing economic, political and social marginalisation? As we noted at the outset of this book, one can see a rise in localist feelings of belonging and growing animosity against 'strangers' in modern-day Africa, as well as elsewhere across the globe. During our writing of this volume, there were many cases of autochthony-inspired violence against 'strangers' (and their reputed allies) around the world, from South Africa to Norway. While such expressions seem to be becoming more common, they do not always result in the kinds of violence that mark these four cases. However, one may well wonder if these four cases are exceptional or harbingers of things to come.

The four countries examined in this book reveal that there is no single cause for autochthony's rise in some parts of modern Africa. In fact, there is enough variation in the cases to give us pause before attempting any sweeping generalisations. Of course, bringing in non-African cases would greatly enrich the investigation of autochthony as a modern phenomenon. Yet a few things can be noted, and, reflecting our organisational strategy in Chapter 2, we conclude this volume by reviewing some of the insights provided by this study.

At the beginning of the book we argued for situating colonialism within the process of 'globalisation'. Indeed, the four cases illustrate that the process of colonialism directly and indirectly contributed to the development of autochthony in modern African politics. Colonial administrative practices, in particular those in 'settler colonies', made what were flexible forms of identity more rigid and politically relevant. They often heralded new ways of thinking about land and land ownership, introducing a legal system that underpinned the privatisation of land, but often in unequal and arbitrary ways. Indeed, in the four cases studied, we can regard the employment of autochthony discourses partly as a rejection of the privileged position of title deeds, while still firmly accepting the logic of land privatisation. In general, under colonialism, identity and land became increasingly intertwined. But while it is important to recognise the legacy of colonialism, one should not overgeneralise or overstate the case. After all, the experience of colonialism in Liberia, where it was conducted by returned American slaves, was substantially different from the experience elsewhere across the continent. Moreover, the other three cases reflect the diversity of colonial strategies employed by the French, Belgian and British. To speak broadly about colonialism often obscures as much as it illuminates.

In addition, colonial policies often reinforced, and in some cases institutionalised, already existing practices and beliefs. The Belgians, for example, did not invent the Hutu/Tutsi categorisation. Likewise, the Americo-Liberian state certainly cemented and partly created ethnic categories around their state structures, but they did not invent the 'stranger-father' institutions nor the lineage relationships between the Loma and the Mandingo in Lofa County. Nor did the French create the Ivorian *tutorat* institution. In these cases, the colonial state continued and strengthened already existing traditions. The break with pre-colonial practices may have been most pronounced in the Kenyan state, largely due to the actions of the settler community, but even there it often worked with pre-existing social relationships and customs. With regards to land, the reality is that, in most cases, land rights issues were already hierarchically organised. Colonialism played into this and exploited it, but colonialism did not create it.

Likewise, conversations about the impact of modern globalisation need to be nuanced. The manifestations of contemporary global economic restructuring vary significantly across the continent, especially given the atomistic nature of global capital. But to understand each of the four cases studied, they need to be viewed against a background of changes within the global political economy. One must locate the outbreak of the Ivorian civil war within the context of the shifting global cocoa market and the effects that economic neoliberalisation had on the state and society in Côte d'Ivoire. Likewise, the political developments in Liberia were intimately linked to regional economic networks that emerged within the context of globalisation. Similarly, one must understand the violence in eastern DRC as being played out against a background in which informal trade networks connected local actors with important international markets. Finally, politics in the post-Kenyatta Kenyan state clearly reflect the effects of economic liberalisation within shifting economic conditions and opportunities. Moreover, all four cases point to the significance of the movement of capital, goods and weapons that characterises modern globalisation, as well as the increased prevalence and importance of communication technologies. Thus, it is highly unlikely that the political conflicts examined in this volume would have taken shape in the ways that they did outside the context of modern globalisation. Yet again, one should not overstate the argument. Globalisation did not cause the rise of autochthony. After all, these are familiar trends taking place across the globe, but a universal rise in autochthony and autochthonous violence has not been seen. The ongoing process of global economic restructuring has acted as a contributive factor, but certainly not a causal one.

A common element in all four cases is the existence of a dysfunctional neopatrimonial state. In fact, the reasons behind the crises in each case can partly be related to globalisation, as shifts in countries' economic fortunes, imposed structural adjustment programmes and political liberalisation (often imposed from the outside) eroded the sustainability of the vertical networks of redistribution so vital for neopatrimonial systems. For example, Kenyatta's and Houphouët-Boigny's successors were unable to maintain their countries' post-colonial compromise largely because of changes in the global political economy. However, one can make a clear distinction between the hollowed-out shadow states of Liberia and DRC and the more 'substantial' and centralised Kenyan state. These are very different states engaging in different state-making processes. Therefore, there are substantial differences between these neopatrimonial systems and their dysfunctionality. What is a common element is the fact that recent crises within neopatrimonialism have altered the established 'rules of the game', providing new opportunities for some political leaders and heightened uncertainty for much of the population.

In the cases of Côte d'Ivoire and Kenya, the outbreak of autochthonous political violence was directly related to political liberalisation. In these cases, the introduction of multiparty elections was clearly a contributing factor in the employment of autochthony as a political strategy. In these, and in other cases, the vertical versus horizontal affiliations that characterise modern African politics did not play out according to liberal assumptions about democratisation, a point that we return to below. But was democratisation the problem? Some authors have used these cases to question the issue of democratisation and democratic sequencing (see Branch and Cheeseman 2008).

Looking at the Kenyan case, Branch and Cheeseman (ibid.: 21) remind us that:

> multi-party elections do not cause violence in any meaningful sense, but they can create incentives for leaders to adopt increasingly antagonistic strategies. Moreover, when such elections are held within a first-past-the-post electoral system, they may encourage a 'winner-takes-all' struggle for control of the state.

Thus, democratisation is not a causal factor per se, but these cases do give one reason to reflect on the forms that political liberalisation and multipartyism can take. In a situation where international forces often uncritically privilege the holding of competitive elections as part of conflict resolution (see the cases of Côte d'Ivoire, Liberia, DRC, Sierra Leone and others), one may be forgiven for worrying that they may cause more harm than good – particularly in a context of hollow institutions and the lack of a clear consensus on who constitutes the polity.

Another common factor in each of these four cases is the key role played by regional big men. In each case, regional big men were instrumental in propagating autochthony discourses and funding the armed militias that engaged in much of the political violence. While important work has recently been done on the role of regional big men in African conflicts (see Utas 2012), we believe that this is a vital field of research. It may be best to regard regional big men as 'fluid nodal points in complex and informal networks of governance and attempts at order' (Bøås 2012b). This is a concept that draws on the work of Marshall Sahlins (1963) on the Melanesian big men, in which authority is personal power. Big men do not come to office; they do not succeed to, nor are they installed in, existing positions of leadership over political groups. The attainment of 'big man' status is rather the outcome of a series of acts that elevate a person above the common herd and attract to him a coterie of loyal, lesser men (ibid.: 289, quoted in Utas 2012: 6). The big man has the ability to command and to instigate mass action. Authority is not structurally ascribed or socio-historically motivated but based on the big man's ability to create a following and is, to a large extent, dependent on his ability to assist people privately.

The role played by regional big men in instigating and sustaining autochthonous violence is important to recognise, because it disrupts _ablished assumptions that autochthony is a grassroots phenomenon of the dispossessed. John Lonsdale (2008a: 307), for example, has argued that: 'A claim to be original, autochthonous, a first-comer, is the weapon, even the refuge, of the weak.' We understand, and agree with, his claim that autochthony provides 'refuge' for the 'weak', as it is similar to our understanding of how autochthony works within the melancholic uncertainty of many marginalised African communities. But the reality is that autochthony as a 'weapon' is primarily the purview of the powerful: the regional big men clinging or aspiring to political rewards. It gains traction because it seemingly offers a strategy for dealing with the melancholic uncertainty of many disadvantaged people. But while, as a strategy, the struggle may be portrayed as collective, the gains are most certainly individual.

This is connected to a realisation regarding the ways in which socio-economic class is experienced in modern African politics. While most explicitly discussed in the Kenyan case study, class is clearly linked to land in much of Africa. The ability to access land is not only a vital aspect of economic survival, even if working the land is not a person's primary economic activity, but also an important marker of class status. Thus, we feel it would be fruitful for scholars to rethink the function of land and landlessness in the making of contemporary identity politics in Africa. Doing so would, at the very least, reintroduce class into the study of African politics, albeit in a different manner than in much of the Marxist-informed scholarship of the past.

Returning to our discussion of regional big men, another significant observation from our comparative study is the effect of the decentral-isation of violence across Africa. Specifically, we are concerned with the rise of private militias. In every case studied in this book, from the Jeunes Patriotes of Côte d'Ivoire to the Kalenjin warriors of Kenya, the majority of autochthony-informed violence was carried out by these private militias and organised gangs. And in every case they enjoyed the support of regional big men. In the Liberian and DRC cases, these armed groups emerged as part of the political strategies that developed the shadow states. As such, they illustrate Robert Bates' (2008) argument that societies militarise against a failing state executive. Yet, as we noted in the chapter on Kenya, African societies have also been militarised *through* the executive. Therefore, we think it is important to recognise a distinction between the autochthonous violence of armed gangs and that of the more general and emotive 'mob violence'. The former is organised purposefully and supported by regional big men as part of a specific political strategy, while the latter is merely fanned by regional big men's autochthonous rhetoric. While it is tempting to conclude that the regional big men have greater control over the former, that may not actually be the case, as the decentralisation of violence has increasingly allowed these armed groups greater autonomy.

Common to both expressions of autochthonous violence is the primacy of young males, who have increasingly found themselves marginalised in African societies. This is a point that we have covered extensively in this volume and elsewhere (see Bøås and Dunn 2007). We will not belabour the point here, except to stress that any sustainable strategy for post-conflict resolution and peace-building must take into consideration ways of addressing the marginalisation of young males (see also Utas 2003). Likewise, the multiple ways in which autochthony discourses and their violent expression reflect and reify gender dynamics need to be recognised. Autochthony claims are almost always grounded in patriarchal practices and assumptions, such as the acceptance that land passes from father to son. This leaves women, who are assumed to be assimilated into the husband's community, more vulnerable to those claims, as well as often being targets of that violence (see Lonsdale 2008a: 307–8).

We conclude with some thoughts about conflict resolution and peace-building in general. Frankly, our investigation into these cases does not fill us with optimism about the likely success of current strategies. Contemporary peacekeeping projects tend to assume the universal validity of a consensus-building approach, based on impartial mediation and negotiations by members of the international community (Woodhouse 2000: 8–25). Andreas Mehler and Denis Tull (2005) observe that power-sharing agreements between insurgents have emerged as the West's preferred instrument of peace-making in Africa. They raise the concern that the institutionalisation of this strategy runs the risk of creating important 'incentive structures' that make violent behaviour increasingly appealing, especially in the pursuit of otherwise blocked political aspirations. The proliferation of armed groups in the Kivus as part of the peace negotiations discussed in Chapter 5 certainly illustrates this point. Moreover, the case of Liberia suggests that some insurgencies may be resistant to resolution by consent and negotiation, resulting in the prolonging of a conflict and an increase in civilian casualties and misery (see Shearer 1997).

Likewise, in his examination of pre-genocide Rwanda, Christopher Clapham (1998) rejects the uncritical promotion of political liberalisation as the cornerstone of western peace-making processes. He notes that two models of conflict resolution have become dominant: the installation of a constitution based on multiparty democracy (for example in Angola and Mozambique) and the creation of a coalition government (attempted in Liberia and Somalia). By looking at the Rwandan case, in which variants of both approaches were applied, leading to disastrous consequences, Clapham suggests that the methods and assumptions in the dominant conflict resolution model are inherently flawed. Specifically, he questions the neoliberal assumptions that conflicting parties share a common value framework, within which differences can be negotiated, and the assumed neutrality and inherent value of mediation. For Clapham, these assumptions helped foster the conditions from which the 1994 Rwandan genocide emerged. Likewise, we raise the same concerns regarding all four of our case studies in this book.

Finally, there is an assumption in contemporary conflict resolution that government institutions need reforming and strengthening. Indeed, there is an uncritical acceptance of the need for a strong state. Even when there is general agreement that the central state is one of the main sources of insecurity among the population – as it was in all four of our cases – externally imposed projects of post-conflict restructuring privilege the strengthening of the state. In her work in post-conflict DRC, for example, Séverine Autesserre (2010) notes that most non-governmental organisations and international actors recognise that the Congolese state is a negative force in most people's lives, yet they continue state-centric notions of reconstruction that work to reinforce the central state and thus increase human insecurity on the ground. Thus, dominant strategies of conflict resolution and rebuilding may end up exacerbating situations in which autochthonous violence is at work.

Of course, the politics of belonging will continue to be a major aspect of life in Africa, as it is elsewhere. People will continue to seek some form of inclusion, inevitably excluding others. People will also continue to lose things that are dear to them and search for explanations that make sense of the loss. They will continue to face uncertainty and insecurity. But there are many options available, and recourse to violent articulations of a politics of origin need not be the most attractive.

The political landscapes in the countries that have constituted our case studies are unfortunately uncertain, but we should also bear in mind that 'uncertainty' does not automatically need to end with a quest for 'dead certainty' and the melancholy of death that will follow in its wake. It can also lead to creativity and the search for home-grown hybrid political order to keep uncertainty under control. This was precisely the reason why the institution of the Liberian 'stranger-father' and the Ivorian *tutorat* were created in the past. They were far from perfect systems and never just, in a modern sense of the word, but for a long time they worked and they produced an order that respected the value of life and dignity. We are not calling for a naive return to tradition in African politics, but we would nonetheless like to point out that institutional innovations have taken place in Africa before and are also happening today. It is not completely unimaginable that new and more inclusive versions of the 'stranger-father' and the *tutorat* can be envisioned as the basis for new social contracts between 'first-comers' and 'latecomers', contracts that could constitute new and productive ways of sharing land and labour.

NOTES

2 African politics

1 Our thanks to Peter Geschiere for helping us sharpen our thinking about this concept.

3 Liberia

1 In 1909, when most non-Americo-Liberians were granted full citizenship, the Mandingo continued to be classified as an 'ethnic minority' (see Konneh 1996).

2 Former members of Samuel Doe's fragmented army and Liberian refugees established ULIMO in Sierra Leone. Most of the original ULIMO fighters were of Krahn and Mandingo origin. Under the leadership of Alhaji Kromah, a Mandingo and a former Doe official, ULIMO first fought in south-eastern Sierra Leone before it battled its way back to Liberia and Lofa County (see also Gberie 2005; Reno 2007).

3 LURD was established in Guinea as a successor to the Mandingo faction in ULIMO just after Taylor's victory in the 1997 elections (see Huband 1998; Ellis 1999; Bøås 2005; Reno 2007).

4 The Poro society is the secret society of the men. It has political, religious and educational responsibilities, and all young men in a community will be initiated into it. As a social organisation it is hierarchically organised and only those initiated into the top circles wield much influence. As such, its political power is best understood as a form of control through ritual hierarchies that reinforce the ability of high-ranking individuals and lineages to command labour and resources (see also Little 1965; Meyer and Moran 2006).

5 Please note that the institution of 'stranger-father' relationships is not unique to Lofa, but is a common institution in most forest societies in the Mano River basin and in Côte d'Ivoire. It goes under many names and some aspects of it may differ, but in essence it is the same.

6 As a consequence of the nature of the war in Lofa, the Loma also formed their own militia, the Lofa Defence Force. It was established in 1993–94 with the support of the Poro society. Its political leader was François Massaquoi (see also Ellis 1999).

7 Konneh (1996: 22) points to oral sources that tell stories about the burning of Mandingo mosques as early as the 1840s. This date may in itself not be very trustworthy, but at least these narratives show how deeply embedded in the collective historical memory this conflict is.

8 Figure 3.1 is based on data from Bøås and Hatløy (2006).

9 The distance between Ganta and the Mandingo towns in Lofa is substantial, but people are remarkably well informed about these events through oral sources. Both the Mandingo in Ganta and those in Lofa trade with Guinea; through their excursions into the Guinée Forestière region and their trade networks, they exchange not only goods but also news. It is quite fascinating to sit in an isolated Mandingo town such as Tusso and listen to people's informed opinions and discussions about the situation in Ganta.

10 See Konneh (1996) for further information concerning the historical

foundation of Mandingo dominance in trade in Ganta.

11 Former LURD fighters have already been (re)mobilised to protect Condé's rule. In crushing the violent street demonstrations in Conakry in January and February 2007, the security forces were assisted by ex-LURD combatants controlled by Aisha Conneh, the former wife of the ex-LURD leader Sekou Conneh.

12 After Samory Touré's defeat in 1898, bands of these former warriors, known as *sofa* from the Mandingo word for horse (as many of them were cavalrymen), roamed the Guinée Forestière region and further into Kpelle territories in what is currently Bong County in Liberia. These young men spread death and destruction, but they also promoted trade and economic opportunities that led other people of Mandingo origin to follow in their footsteps (see Konneh 1996).

4 Kenya

1 As in English-speaking Liberia, the term 'autochthony' is not part of the Kenyan political discourse. Instead, one finds reference to 'indigenous' and 'native', yet the issues and processes are the same.

2 It should be noted that there was substantial tension among the Kikuyu over these allocations, as the Kenyatta government seems to have actively excluded former Mau Mau supporters from scheme allocations, instead privileging the Kikuyu 'loyalists' who had fought against the Mau Mau (Leo 1984).

3 Based on their survey data, Bratton and Kimenyi (2008: 276) argue that Kenyans tend to downplay their own ethnicity, but express strong distrust of fellow Kenyans hailing from different ethnic groups. In general, they assume that other ethnic groups are more prone to political conflict, organise politically

along exclusive ethnic lines, and govern in a discriminatory fashion.

5 Democratic Republic of Congo

1 Congo has vast natural resources. Among the most important are bauxite/ aluminium, cadmium, cassiterite, coal, cobalt, copper, coltan, diamonds, gas, gold, iron ore, lead, manganese, oil, silver, timber, uranium and zinc.

2 Kabila was re-elected in 2011, defeating Etienne Tshisekedi in a vote that few observers considered either free or fair.

3 This figure is quite uncertain, and other studies have come up with much lower figures, but all show very high mortality figures particularly in the eastern parts of the country.

4 MONUSCO took over from the earlier peacekeeping operation – the United Nations Organisation Mission in the Democratic Republic of Congo (MONUC) on 1 July 2010. This was done in accordance with Security Council Resolution 1925 of 28 May 2010, but the main reason was to suit the Kabila government argument that the civil war was over.

5 Conservationists working in Virunga National Park have estimated that the charcoal market may be worth as much as US $30 million a year (see Stearns 2011).

6 Côte d'Ivoire

1 These three groups were the Mouvement Patriotique de Côte d'Ivoire (MPCI), Mouvement Populaire Ivoirien du Grand Ouest (MPIGO) and Mouvement pour la Justice et la Paix (MJP).

2 Portions of this chapter are drawn from Bøås and Huser (2006).

3 These groups are usually categorised into the following five cultural and linguistic clusters: Akan, Seoufo, Mande North and South, and Krou. Even

the largest group, the Akan-speaking Baoulé, accounts for approximately only 20 per cent of the population.

4 Kieffer was last seen being driven away by uniformed men after telling his friends he had received death threats. It is widely believed that Michel Legré, the brother-in-law of President Laurent Gbagbo's wife, was involved in Kieffer's disappearance and most likely murder (see BBC, 15 June 2004).

5 The Dozo (or Donzo, which in Bambara means hunter) are traditional hunters who live in northern Côte d'Ivoire, south-east Mali and Burkina Faso. They do not constitute an ethnic group, but are a hunter guild that exists in Mande-speaking and Dyula communities in this part of West Africa. Encompassing a blend of practical skills and magical abilities, Dozo groups have increased in number as well as prominence during the Ivorian civil war (see Hellweg 2011).

BIBLIOGRAPHY

Abrams, P. D. (1979) *Kenya's Land Resettlement Story*. Nairobi: Challenge Publishers.

Afoaku, Osita (2002) 'Congo rebels: their origins, motivations and strategies', in John F. Clark (ed.) *The African Stakes of the Congo War*. New York, NY: Palgrave Macmillan. pp. 109–28.

Anderson, David and Emma Lochery (2008) 'Violence and exodus in Kenya's Rift Valley, 2008: predictable and preventable?' *Journal of Eastern African Studies*, vol. 2, no. 2, pp. 328–43.

Appadurai, Arjun (1999) 'Dead certainty: ethnic violence in the era of globalization', in Birgit Meyer and Peter Geschiere (eds) *Globalization and Identity: Dialectics of flow and closure*. Oxford: Blackwell Publishers. pp. 305–24.

Autesserre, Séverine (2010) *The Trouble with the Congo: Local violence and the failure of international peacebuilding*. Cambridge: Cambridge University Press.

Banégas, Richard and Ruth Marshall-Fratani (2003) 'Côte d'Ivoire, un conflit régional?: La Côte d'Ivoire en guerre: dynamiques du dedans et du dehors'. *Politique Africaine*, vol. 89, pp. 5–11.

— (2007) 'Côte d'Ivoire: negotiating identity and citizenship', in Morten Bøås and Kevin C. Dunn (eds) *African Guerrillas: Raging against the machine*. Boulder, CO: Lynne Rienner. pp. 81–112.

Bates, Robert H. (2008) *When Things Fell Apart: State failure in late-centruy*

Africa. Cambridge: Cambridge University Press.

Bauman, Zygmunt (1991) *Modernity and Ambivalence*. Cambridge: Polity Press.

Bayart, Jean-François, Peter Geschiere and Francis B. Nyamnjoh (2001) 'Autochtonie, démocratie et citoyenneté en Afrique'. *Critique Internationale*, vol. 10, pp. 177–94.

BBC (2004) 'Man charged over Ivorian kidnap'. London: BBC Africa. 15 June.

— (2011) 'Gbagbo supporters "outraged" at transfer'. London: BBC Africa. 30 November.

Berdal, Mats and David M. Malone (eds) (2000) *Greed and Grievance: Economic agendas in civil wars*. Boulder, CO: Lynne Rienner.

Berman, Bruce and John Lonsdale (1992) *Unhappy Valley: Conflict in Kenya and Africa*. Books 1 and 2. Athens, OH: Ohio University Press.

Bøås, Morten (2005) 'The Liberian civil war: new war/old war?' *Global Society*, vol. 19, no. 1, pp. 73–88.

— (2008) '"Just another day": the North Kivu security predicament after the 2006 Congolese elections'. *African Security*, vol. 1, no. 1, pp. 53–68.

— (2009a) '"New" nationalism and autochthony: tales of origin as political cleavage'. *Africa Spectrum*, vol. 44, no. 1, pp. 19–38.

— (2009b) 'Funérailles pour un ami: des luttes de citoyenneté dans la guerre civile libérienne'. *Politique Africaine*, no. 112, pp. 36–51.

— (2009c) 'Making plans for Liberia: a trusteeship approach to good governance?' *Third World Quarterly*, vol. 30, no. 7, pp. 1329–41.

— (2010) 'Returning to realities: a building-block approach to state and statecraft in Eastern Congo and Somalia'. *Conflict, Security & Development*, vol. 10, no. 4, pp. 443–64.

— (2012a) 'Autochthony and citizenship: "civil society" as vernacular architecture?' *Journal of Intervention and Statebuilding*, vol. 6, no. 1, pp. 91–105.

— (2012b) '"Castles in the sand": informal networks and power brokers in the northern Mali periphery', in Mats Utas (ed.) *African Conflicts and Informal Power: Big men and networks*. London: Zed Books. pp. 119–34.

Bøås, Morten and Kevin C. Dunn (eds) (2007) *African Guerrillas: Raging against the machine*. Boulder, CO: Lynne Rienner.

Bøås, Morten and Anne Hatløy (2006) *After the 'Storm': Economic activities among returning youths. The case of Voinjama*. Fafo Report 523. Oslo: Fafo.

— (2008) '"Getting in, getting out": militia membership and prospects for re-integration in post-war Liberia'. *Journal of Modern African Studies*, vol. 46, no. 1, pp. 33–55.

Bøås, Morten and Anne Huser (2006) *Child Labour and Cocoa Production in West Africa: The case of Côte d'Ivoire and Ghana*. Fafo Report 522. Oslo: Fafo.

Bøås, Morten and Mats Utas (2013) *The Political Landscape of Post-war Liberia: Historical dividing lines and the 2011 elections*. (Forthcoming.)

Bohannan, Paul and Philip D. Curtin (1995) *Africa and Africans*. Prospect Heights, IL: Waveland Press.

Boone, Catherine (2003) *Political Topographies of the African State: Territorial authority and institutional choice*. Cambridge: Cambridge University Press.

Boserup, Ester (1976) 'Environment, population and technology in primitive societies'. *Population and Development Review*, vol. 2, no. 1, pp. 21–36.

Braathen, Einar, Morten Bøås, and Gjermund Sæther (eds) (2000) *Ethnicity Kills? The politics of war, peace and ethnicity in Sub-Saharan Africa*. London: Palgrave Macmillan.

Braeckman, Colette (2003) *Les Nouveaux Prédateurs: politique des puissances en Afrique centrale*. Paris: Fayard.

Branch, Daniel (2009) *Defeating Mau Mau, Creating Kenya: Counterinsurgency, civil war, and decolonization*. Cambridge: Cambridge University Press.

Branch, Daniel and Nic Cheeseman (2008) 'Democratization, sequencing, and state failure in Africa: lessons from Kenya'. *African Affairs*, vol. 108, no. 430, pp. 1–26.

Bratton, Michael and Mwangi S. Kimenyi (2008) 'Voting in Kenya: putting ethnicity in perspective'. *Journal of Eastern African Studies*, vol. 2, no. 2, pp. 272–89.

Bratton, Michael and Daniel N. Posner (1999) 'A first look at second elections in Africa, with illustrations from Zambia', in Richard Joseph (ed.) *State, Conflict, and Democracy in Africa*. Boulder, CO: Lynne Rienner. pp. 377–407.

Bustin, Edouard (1999) 'The collapse of "Congo/Zaïre" and its regional impact', in Daniel Bach (ed.) *Regionalisation in Africa: Integration and disintegration*. London/Bloomington, IN: James Currey/Indiana University Press. pp. 81–90.

Chappell, David A. (1989) 'The nation as frontier: ethnicity and clientelism in Ivorian history'. *International Journal of African Historical Studies*, vol. 22, no. 4, pp. 671–96.

Chauveau, Jean-Pierre and Jean-Pierre

Dozon (1987) 'Au coeur des ethnies ivoiriennes... l'État', in Emmanuel Terray (ed.) *L'État Contemporain en Afrique*. Paris: L'Hamattan. pp. 221–96.

Cheeseman, Nic (2008) 'The Kenyan elections of 2007: an introduction'. *Journal of Eastern African Studies*, vol. 2, no. 2, pp. 166–84.

Clapham, Christopher (1998) 'Rwanda: The perils of peacemaking'. *Journal of Peace Research*, vol. 25, no. 2, pp. 193–210.

Clark, Ian (1997) *Globalization and Fragmentation: International relations in the twentieth century*. Oxford: Oxford University Press.

Clark, John F. (ed.) (2002) *The African Stakes of the Congo War*. New York, NY: Palgrave Macmillan.

Colin, Jean-Philippe, Georges Kouamé and Débégnoun Soro (2007) 'Outside the autochthon-migrant configuration: access to land, land conflicts and inter-ethnic relationships in a former pioneer area of lower Côte d'Ivoire'. *Journal of Modern African Studies*, vol. 45, no. 1, pp. 33–59.

Collier, Paul (2000) *Economic Causes of Civil Conflict and Their Implications for Policy*. Washington, DC: World Bank.

— (2007) *The Bottom Billion: Why the poorest countries are failing and what can be done about it*. Oxford: Oxford University Press.

Collins, Carole J. L. (1997) 'Reconstructing the Congo'. *Review of African Political Economy*, vol. 24, no. 74, pp. 591–600.

Cosma, Wilungula B. (1997) *Fizi 1967– 1986: Le Maquis Kabila*. Brussels: Centre d'Étude et de Documentation Africaines (CEDAF).

Crook, Richard C. (1997) 'Winning coalitions and ethno-regional politics: the failure of the opposition in the 1990 and 1995 elections in Côte d'Ivoire'. *African Affairs*, vol. 96, no. 383, pp. 215–42.

D'Azevedo, Warren L. (1962) 'Some historical problems in the delineation of a central west Atlantic region'. *Anthropology and Africa Today*, vol. 96, pp. 512–38.

Daily Nation (2008) 'Kivuitu calls for probe into tallying of presidential votes'. 3 January.

de Boeck, Filip (1996) 'Postcolonialism, power and identity: local and global perspectives from Zaïre', in Richard Werbner and Terence Ranger (eds) *Postcolonial Identities in Africa*. London: Zed Books.

de Smedt, Johan (2009) '"No Raila, no peace!": big man politics and election violence at the Kibera grassroots'. *African Affairs*, vol. 108, no. 433, pp. 581–98.

de St Moulin, L. (1990) 'What is known of the demographic history of Zaire since 1885?' In Bruce Fetter (ed.) *Demography from Scanty Evidence: Central Africa in the colonial era*. Boulder, CO: Lynne Rienner. pp. 299–325.

de Waal, Alex (2007) *War in Darfur and the Search for Peace*. Cambridge, MA: Harvard University Press.

Derman, Bill, Rie Odgaard and Espen Sjaastad (2007) 'Introduction', in Bill Derman, Rie Odgaard and Espen Sjaastad (eds) *Conflicts over Land and Water in Africa*. Oxford: James Currey. pp. 1–30.

Dian, Boni (1985) *L'Économie de Plantation en Côte-d'Ivoire Forestière*. Abidjan: Nouvelles Editions Africaines.

Doty, Roxanne Lynn (2003) *Anti-Immigrantism in Western Democracies: Statecraft, desire and the politics of exclusion*. London: Routledge.

Dozon, Jean-Pierre (1985) 'Les Bété: une création coloniale', in J.-L. Amselle and E. M'Bokolo (eds) *Au Coeur de l'Ethnie: Ethnies, tribalisme et état en Afrique*. Paris: La Découverte. pp. 49–85.

Duffield, Mark (2001) *Global Governance and the New Wars: The merging of development and security*. London: Zed Books.

Dunn, Kevin C. (2002) 'A survival guide to Kinshasa: lessons of the father, passed down to the son', in John F. Clark (ed.) *The African Stakes of the Congo War*. New York, NY: Palgrave Macmillan. pp. 53–74.

— (2003) *Imagining the Congo: The international relations of identity*. New York, NY: Palgrave Macmillan.

— (2009) '"Sons of the soil" and contemporary state making: autochthony, uncertainty and political violence in Africa'. *Third World Quarterly*, vol. 30, no. 1, pp. 113–27.

— (2010) 'There is no such thing as the state: discourse, effect and performativity'. *Forum for Development Studies*, vol. 37, no. 1, pp. 79–92.

Ellis, Stephen (1998) 'Liberia's warlord insurgency', in Christopher Clapham (ed.) *African Guerrillas*. Oxford: James Currey. pp. 155–71.

— (1999) *The Mask of Anarchy: The destruction of Liberia and the religious dimensions of an African civil war*. London: C. Hurst & Company.

European Union Election Observation Mission (EOM) (2008) 'Preliminary statement: doubts about the credibility of the presidential results hamper Kenya's democratic progress'. 1 January. Available at www.europarl.europa.eu/meetdocs/2004_2009/documents/dv/afet-21jano8kenya eomprelconclusio/afet-21jano8kenya eomprelconclusions.pdf.

Evans, Glynne (1997) *Responding to Crises in the African Great Lakes*. Adelphi Paper 311. Oxford: Oxford University Press.

Fanon, Frantz (1965) *The Wretched of the Earth*. New York, NY: Grove Press.

Forbath, Peter (1977) *The River Congo*. New York, NY: Harper and Row.

Freud, Sigmund (1913) *Totem and Taboo* (translated by A. A. Brill). New York, NY: Moffat, Yard & Co.

Gberie, Lansana (2005) *A Dirty War in West Africa: The RUF and the destruction of Sierra Leone*. Bloomington, IN: Indiana University Press.

Gerard-Libois, J. and Benoit Verhaegen (1961) *Congo 1960*. Brussels: Centre de Recherche et d'Information Socio-Politiques (CRISP).

Geschiere, Peter (2004) 'Ecology, belonging and xenophobia: the 1994 forest law in Cameroon and the issue of "community"', in Harri Englund and Francis B. Nyamnjoh (eds) *Rights and the Politics of Recognition in Africa*. London: Zed Books. pp. 237–59.

— (2009) *Perils of Belonging: Autochthony, citizenship, and exclusion in Africa and Europe*. Chicago, IL: University of Chicago Press.

Geschiere, Peter and Stephen Jackson (2006) 'Autochthony and the crisis of citizenship: democratization, decentralization, and the politics of belonging'. *African Studies Review*, vol. 49, no. 2, pp. 1–7.

Geschiere, Peter and Francis B. Nyamnjoh (2000) 'Capitalism and autochthony: the seesaw of mobility and belonging'. *Public Culture*, vol. 12, no. 2, pp. 423–52.

Guyer, David (1970) *Ghana and the Ivory Coast: The impact of colonialism in an African setting*. New York, NY: Exposition Press.

Hagberg, Sten (2004) 'Ethnic identification in voluntary associations: the politics of development and culture in Burkina Faso', in Harri Englund and Francis B. Nyamnjoh (eds) *Rights and the Politics of Recognition in Africa*. London: Zed Books. pp. 195–218.

Hara, Fabienne and Comfort Ero (2002) *Ivory Coast on the Brink*. Freetown/Brussels: International Crisis Group.

Harneit-Sievers, Axel and Ralph-Michael Peters (2008) 'Kenya's 2007 general election and its aftershocks'. *Afrika Spectrum*, vol. 43, no. 1, pp. 133–44.

Hellweg, Joseph (2011) *Hunting the Ethical State: The Benkadi Movement of Côte d'Ivoire.* Chicago, IL: University of Chicago Press.

Hochschild, Adam (1998) *King Leopold's Ghost.* Boston, MA: Houghton Mifflin.

Hodgkin, Thomas (1956) *Nationalism in Colonial Africa.* London: Frederick Muller.

Højbjerg, Christian Kordt (2007) *Resisting State Iconoclasm among the Loma of Guinea.* Durham, NC: Carolina Academic Press.

Homer-Dixon, Thomas (1994) 'Environmental scarcities and violent conflict'. *International Security*, vol. 19, no. 1, pp. 5–40.

— (1999) *Environment, Scarcity, and Violence.* Princeton, NJ: Princeton University Press.

Homer-Dixon, Thomas and Jessica Blitt (eds) (1998) *Ecoviolence: Links among environment, population, and security.* Lanham, MD: Rowman & Littlefield.

Hoskyns, Catherine (1965) *The Congo Since Independence.* Oxford: Oxford University Press.

HRW (2008) *Ballots to Bullets: Organized political violence and Kenya's crisis of governance.* New York, NY: Human Rights Watch (HRW).

Huband, Mark (1998) *The Liberian Civil War.* London: Frank Cass.

Huggins, Chris and Jenny Clover (eds) (2005) *From the Ground Up: Land rights, conflict and peace in sub-Saharan Africa.* Pretoria: Institute for Security Studies (ISS).

Hugon, Anne (1993) *The Exploration of Africa: From Cairo to the Cape.* New York, NY: Abrams.

ICG (2003) *Liberia: Security challenges.* Freetown/Brussels: International Crisis Group (ICG).

— (2004) *Côte d'Ivoire: No peace in sight.* Dakar/Brussels: International Crisis Group (ICG).

— (2005) *Liberia's Elections: Necessary but not sufficient.* Dakar/Brussels: International Crisis Group (ICG).

— (2008) *Kenya in Crisis.* Brussels: International Crisis Group (ICG).

International Criminal Court (ICC) (2011) 'Laurent Gbagbo in ICC custody'. 30 November. Available at www.hague justiceportal.net/index.php?id=13007.

IRC (2007) *Mortality in the Democratic Republic of Congo: An ongoing crisis.* New York, NY: International Rescue Committee (IRC).

Jackson, Stephen (2006) 'Sons of which soil? The language and politics of autochthony in Eastern D.R. Congo'. *African Studies Review*, vol. 49, no. 2, pp. 95–123.

— (2007) 'Of "doubtful nationality": political manipulation of citizenship in the D.R. Congo'. *Citizenship Studies*, vol. 11, no. 5, pp. 481–500.

Juma, Calestous (1996) in Calestous Juma and J. B. Ojwang (eds) *In Land We Trust: Environment, private property and constitutional change.* London: Zed Books.

Kahl, Colin (2006) *States, Scarcity and Civil Strife in the Developing World.* Princeton, NJ: Princeton University Press.

Kaldor, Mary (1999) *New and Old Wars: Organized violence in a global era.* Cambridge: Polity Press.

Kaplan, Robert D. (1994) 'The coming anarchy'. *Atlantic Monthly*, February, pp. 44–76.

Kelly, Sean (1993) *America's Tyrant: The CIA and Mobutu of Zaire.* Washington, DC: American University Press.

Kenya Elections Domestic Observation Forum (KEDOF) (2007) 'Preliminary press statement and verdict of 2007 Kenya's general election'. 31 December. Available at http://kenyastock

holm.files.wordpress.com/2008/01/
kedof-statement-31-12-07.pdf.

Kenya National Commission on Human
Rights (KNCHR) (2007) *Still Behaving
Badly: Second periodic report of the
election-monitoring project*. December. Available at http://cbrayton.
files.wordpress.com/2008/01/
election_report.pdf.

Klare, Michael T. (2001) *Resource
Wars: The new landscape of global
conflict*. New York, NY: Henry Holt &
Company.

Klopp, Jacqueline M. (2000) 'Pilfering
the public: the problem of land
grabbing in contemporary Kenya'.
Africa Today, vol. 47, no. 1, pp. 7–26.

— (2008) 'The real reason for Kenya's
violence'. *Christian Science Monitor*.
14 January.

Konneh, Augustine (1996) *Religion,
Commerce, and the Integration of the
Mandingo in Liberia*. Lanham, MD:
University Press of America.

Kopytoff, Igor (1987) 'The internal African frontier: the making of African
political culture', in Igor Kopytoff
(ed.) *The African Frontier: The reproduction of traditional African societies*.
Bloomington, IN: Indiana University
Press. pp. 3–83.

Lemarchand, René (1998) 'Genocide in
the Great Lakes: Which genocide?
Whose genocide?' *African Studies
Review*, vol. 41, no. 1, pp. 3–16.

— (2008) *The Dynamics of Violence
in Central Africa*. Philadelphia, PA:
University of Pennsylvania Press.

Leo, Christopher (1984) *Land and Class in
Kenya*. Toronto: University of Toronto
Press.

Leys, Colin (1975) *Underdevelopment
in Kenya: The political economy of
underdevelopment 1964–71*. London:
Heinemann.

Li, Tania Murray (2000) 'Articulating
indigenous identity in Indonesia:
resource politics and the tribal slot'.

*Comparative Studies in Society and
History*, vol. 42, no. 1, pp. 149–79.

Liebenow, J. Gus (1987) *Liberia: The
Quest for Democracy*. Bloomington,
IN: Indiana University Press.

Lietzmann, Kurt M. and Gary D. Vest
(1999) 'Environment and security in
an international context: executive
summary report. NATO/Committee
on the Challenges of Modern Society
Pilot Study'. *Environmental Change
and Security Project Report*, issue 5,
pp. 34–48.

Little, Kenneth (1965) *West African
Urbanization*. Cambridge: Cambridge
University Press.

Lonsdale, John (2008a) 'Soil, work,
civilisation, and citizenship in Kenya'.
Journal of Eastern African Studies,
vol. 2, no. 2, pp. 305–14.

— (2008b) 'Kenya: ethnicity, tribe, and
state'. *Pambazuka News*, issue 338.
Available at http://pambazuka.org/
en/category/comment/45594.

Losch, Bruno, Guy-André Kieffer et al.
(2000) 'Côte d'Ivoire, la tentation
ethnonationaliste'. *Politique Africaine*,
vol. 78, pp. 5–156.

Lynch, Gabrielle (2006) 'Negotiating
ethnicity: identity politics in contemporary Kenya'. *Review of African
Political Economy*, vol. 33, no. 107,
pp. 49–65.

— (2008) 'Courting the Kalenjin:
the failure of dynasticism and the
strength of the ODM wave in Kenya's
Rift Valley province'. *African Affairs*,
vol. 107, no. 429, pp. 541–68.

Malkki, Liisa (1995) *Purity and Exile:
Violence, memory, and national
cosmology among Hutu refugees in
Tanzania*. Chicago, IL: University of
Chicago Press.

Maloba, Wunyabari (1998) *Mau Mau and
Kenya: An analysis of a peasant revolt*.
Bloomington, IN: Indiana University
Press.

Mamdani, Mahmood (2001) *When Victims*

Become Killers: Colonialism, nativism, and the genocide in Rwanda. Princeton, NJ: Princeton University Press.

— (2002) 'African states, citizenship and war: a case study'. *International Affairs*, vol. 78, no. 2, pp. 493–506.

Marshall-Fratani, Ruth (2006) 'The war of "who is who"; autochthony, nationalism, and citizenship in the Ivoirian crisis'. *African Studies Review*, vol. 49, no. 2, pp. 9–43.

Massey, D. (2005) *For Space*. London: Sage Publications.

Mathieu, Paul and Mafikiri Tsongo (1998) 'Guerres paysannes au Nord-Kivu, 1937–1994'. *Cahiers d'Études Africaines*, vol. 38, no. 150–2, pp. 385–416.

Mbembe, Achille (1992) 'Provisional notes on the postcolony'. *Africa: Journal of the International African Institute*, vol. 62, no. 1, pp. 3–37.

— (2001) *On the Postcolony*. Berkeley, CA: University of California Press.

McGovern, Mike (2011) *Making War in Côte d'Ivoire*. London: C. Hurst & Company.

McNulty, Mel (1999) 'The collapse of Zaïre: implosion, revolution or external sabotage?' *Journal of Modern African Studies*, vol. 37, no. 1, pp. 53–82.

Médard, Claire (2008a) 'Elected leaders, militias and prophets: violence in Mount Elgon (2006–2008)'. *Les Cahiers d'Afrique de l'Est*, vol. 37, pp. 349–70.

— (2008b) 'Key issues in disentangling the Kenyan crisis: evictions, autochthony and land privatization'. *Les Cahiers d'Afrique de l'Est*, vol. 37, pp. 375–91.

Médard, Jean-François (1991) 'L'État néopatrimonial en Afrique noire', in Jean-François Médard (ed.) *États d'Afrique Noire*. Paris: Karthala. pp. 323–54.

Mehler, Andreas and Denis M. Tull (2005) 'The hidden costs of power-sharing: reproducing insurgent violence in Africa'. *African Affairs*, vol. 104, no. 416, pp. 375–98.

Meyer, Birgit and Peter Geschiere (1999) 'Introduction', in Birgit Meyer and Peter Geschiere (eds) *Globalization and Identity: Dialectics of flow and closure*. Oxford: Blackwell. pp 1–16.

Meyer, Birgit and Mary H. Moran (2006) *Liberia: The violence of democracy*. Philadelphia, PA: University of Pennsylvania Press.

Murphy, William P. (1980) 'Secret knowledge as property and power in Kpelle society: elders versus youth'. *Africa: Journal of the International African Institute*, vol. 50, no. 2, pp. 193–207.

Newbury, David (1998) 'Understanding genocide'. *African Studies Review*, vol. 41, no. 1, pp. 73–97.

Nguessan-Zoukou, L. (1990) *Régions et Régionalisation en Côte d'Ivoire*. Paris: L'Harmattan.

Njanga, Canda-Ciri (1979) 'La secte Binji-Binji ou la renaissance de la résistance des Bashi (juillet–septembre 1931)' in *Lyangombe, Mythe et Rites*. Bukavu, Congo: CERUKI.

Nwokedi, Emeka (1999) 'On democratic renewal in Francophone West Africa', in Dele Oluwu, Adebayo Williams and Kayode Soremekun (eds) *Governance and Democratisation in West Africa*. Dakar: Council for the Development of Social Science Research in Africa (CODESRIA). pp. 265–86.

O'Brien, Conor Cruise (1966) 'The United Nations and the Congo'. *Studies on the Left*, vol. 6, no. 3.

Osborn, Michelle (2008) 'Fuelling the flames: rumour and politics in Kibera'. *Journal of Eastern African Studies*, vol. 2, no. 2, pp. 315–27.

Person, Yves (1982) 'Islam et décolonisation en Côte d'Ivoire'. *Le Mois en Afrique: Revue Française d'Études Politiques Africaines*, no. 188–9, pp. 15–30.

Pole Institute (2003) *Democratic Republic of Congo: Peace tomorrow?* Goma, Congo: Pole Institute.

Prunier, Gérard (1997) 'The Great Lakes Crisis'. *Current History*, vol. 96, no. 610, pp. 193–9.

— (2008) *Africa's World War: Congo, the Rwandan genocide, and the making of a continental catastrophe*. Oxford: Oxford University Press.

Raeymaekers, Timothy (2007) 'Sharing the spoils: the reinvigoration of Congo's political system'. *Politorbis: Zeitschrift zur Aussenpolitik*, vol. 42, no. 1, pp. 27–33.

Rasmussen, Jacob (2010) 'Outwitting the professor of politics? Mungiki narratives of political deception and their role in Kenyan politics'. *Journal of Eastern African Studies*, vol. 4, no. 3, pp. 435–49.

Reno, William (1997) 'Sovereignty and personal rule in Zaïre'. *African Studies Quarterly*, vol. 1, no. 3. Available at www.africa.ufl.edu/asq/v1/3/4.htm.

— (1998) *Warlord Politics and African States*. Boulder, CO: Lynne Rienner.

— (2007) 'Liberia: The LURDs of the New Church', in Morten Bøås and Kevin C. Dunn (eds) *African Guerrillas: Raging against the machine*. Boulder, CO: Lynne Rienner. pp. 69–80.

Richards, Paul (1996) *Fighting for the Rain Forest: War, youth and resources in Sierra Leone*. Oxford: James Currey.

Richards, Paul et al. (2005) *Community Cohesion in Liberia: A post-war rapid social assessment*. Washington, DC: United Nations Development Programme (UNDP)/World Bank.

Ruf, François (2001) 'Tree crops as deforestation and reforestation agents: the case of coca in Côte d'Ivoire and Sulawesi', in A. Angelsen and D. Kaimowitz (eds) *Agricultural Technologies and Tropical Deforestation*. New York, NY: CABI Publishing. pp. 291–315.

Sahlins, Marshall (1963) 'Poor man, rich man, big-man, chief: political types in Melanesia and Polynesia'. *Comparative Studies in Society and History*, vol. 5, no. 3, pp. 285–303.

Sanders, Edith R. (1969) 'The Hamitic hypothesis: its origin and functions in time perspective'. *Journal of African History*, vol. 10, no. 4, pp. 521–32.

Schatzberg, Michael G. (1991) *Mobutu or Chaos? The United States and Zaire, 1960–1990*. Lanham, MD: University Press of America.

Shearer, David (1997) 'Exploring the limits of consent: conflict resolution in Sierra Leone'. *Millennium*, vol. 26, no. 3, pp. 845–60.

Spear, Thomas and Richard Waller (eds) (1993) *Being Maasai: Ethnicity and identity in East Africa*. Athens, OH: Ohio University Press.

Spittaels, Steven and Filip Hilgert (2008) *Mapping Conflict Motives: Eastern DRC*. Antwerp: International Peace Information Service (IPIS)/Fatal Transactions.

Stearns, Jason K. (2011) *Dancing in the Glory of Monsters: The collapse of the Congo and the Great War of Africa*. New York, NY: PublicAffairs.

Temin, Jonathan (2004) 'Building & sustaining stability in Lofa County, Liberia'. *Review of African Political Economy*, vol. 31, no. 102, pp. 711–15.

Turner, Thomas (1997) 'Kabila returns, in a cloud of uncertainty'. *African Studies Quarterly*, vol. 1, no. 3. Available at www.africa.ufl.edu/asq/v1/3/3.htm.

— (2007) *The Congo Wars: Conflict, myth and reality*. London: Zed Books.

Utas, Mats (2003) *Sweet Battlefields: Youth and the Liberian civil war*. Uppsala: Uppsala University Dissertations in Cultural Anthropology.

— (ed.) (2012) *African Conflicts and Informal Power: Big men and networks*. London: Zed Books.

Vansina, Jan (1966) *Kingdoms of the Savanna*. Madison, WI: University of Wisconsin Press.

— (1990) *Paths in the Rainforests: Toward a history of political tradition in Equatorial Africa*. Oxford: James Currey.

— (2004) *Antecedents to Modern Rwanda: The Nyiginya Kingdom*. Oxford: James Currey.

Vlassenroot, Koen (2002) 'Citizenship, identity formation and conflict in South Kivu: the case of the Banyamulenge'. *Review of African Political Economy*, vol. 29, no. 93–4, pp. 499–515.

Vlassenroot, Koen and Chris Huggins (2005) 'Land, migration and conflict in eastern DRC', in Huggins, Chris and Jenny Clover (eds) *From the Ground Up: Land rights, conflict and peace in sub-Saharan Africa*. Pretoria: Institute for Security Studies (ISS). pp. 115–94.

Vlassenroot, Koen and Timothy Raeymaekers (2009) 'Kivu's intractable security conundrum'. *African Affairs*, vol. 108, no. 432, pp. 475–84.

Watson, Elizabeth E. (2010) 'A "hardening of lines": landscape, religion and identity in northern Kenya'. *Journal of Eastern African Studies*, vol. 4, no. 2, pp. 201–20.

Willame, Jean-Claude (1997) *Banyarwanda et Banyamulenge: Violences ethniques et gestion de l'identitaire au Kivu*. Paris: L'Harmattan.

Woodhouse, Tom (2000) 'Conflict resolution and peacekeeping: critiques and responses', in Tom Woodhouse and Oliver Ramsbotham (eds) *Peacekeeping and Conflict Resolution*. London: Frank Cass.

World Bank (2003) *Land Policies for Growth and Poverty Reduction*. Washington, DC: World Bank/Oxford University Press.

Young, Crawford (1994) *The African Colonial State in Comparative Perspective*. New Haven, CT: Yale University Press.

Žižek, Slavoj (1989) *The Sublime Object of Ideology*. London: Verso Books.

Zolberg, Aristide R. (1964) *One-Party Government in the Ivory Coast*. Princeton, NJ: Princeton University Press.

INDEX

Ntaryamira, Cyprien, 83
Ntimana, William ole, 67
Nyamnjoh, Francis B., 21, 27–8
Nyiginya kingdom, 97

Odgard, R., 7
Odinga, Raila, 52–3, 54, 55, 56, 65, 67, 74
ontological crises, production of, 20
Orange Democratic Movement (ODM)
    (Kenya), 52–6, 60, 66–9
Orange Democratic Movement-Kenya
    (ODM-K), 52
Organisation for Economic Co-operation
    and Development (OECD), 'Helping
    Prevent Violent Conflict', 7
Osborn, Michelle, 67
Other, 34; redefinition of, 27
Ouattara, Alassane, 118, 105, 116, 119,
    120, 122

Parti Démocratique de Côte d'Ivoire
    (PDCI), 103, 105
Parti Ivorien des Travailleurs (Côte
    d'Ivoire), 115
Party of National Unity (PNU) (Kenya),
    52, 66, 68
Patassé, Ange-Félix, 91
patrimonialism, 119
Patriotes Résistants Congolais
    (PARECO), 98, 99, 100, 101
peacekeeping projects, 129
plantation economy, 110, 111, 113; in USA,
    34
population control programmes, 87
post-colonialism, 9
privatisation: of African state, 25; of
    land, 57, 124

Raeymaekers, Timothy, 99
Rassemblement Congolaise pour la
    Démocratie (RCD), 91, 92, 98
Rassemblement des Forces
    Démocratiques de Guinée (RFDG), 37
Rassemblement des Républicains (RDR)
    (Côte d'Ivoire), 103
Red Rubber campaign, 80
Reno, William, 36
resource scarcity, and armed conflict, 3–5

resource wars, 3, 5
Revolutionary United Front (RUF) (Sierra
    Leone), 38, 109
Rift Valley (Kenya), 56
right to stand for election, 11
right to vote, 11
rights to land, 11, 46, 51, 78, 88, 90, 102,
    113, 118, 122
rumour, used as tool, 67
Ruto, William, 60, 61, 65–6, 67, 74–5
Rwanda, 7, 22, 85, 86, 96, 130; cattle
    industry in, 100–1; genocide in, 14,
    89, 93, 130
Rwandan Patriotic Front (RPF), 83, 97,
    98
Rwandophones, 98–101

Sabaot, use of term, 73
Sabaot Land Defence Force (SLDF), 73
Sahlins, Marshall, 127
Sang, Joshua arap, 74
Seimavileh, 43
Shaba province, 84
Sheriff, Aliyu, 41–2, 51
Sierra Leone, 38
Sirleaf, Ellen Johnson, 39, 48
Sjaastad, E., 7
Somalia, 130
Soro, Guillaume, 119
South Africa, 81
sovereignty, discourses of, 20
Stanley, Henry Morton, 77, 78; known as
    Bula Matari, 80
state: African (nature of, 19–24;
    privatisation of, 25); as political
    arena, 33; inexistence of, 20;
    state-making processes, 31, 32, 126;
    weakening of, 32; Westphalian model
    of, 23
stateless spaces, 56
stranger, 28, 32, 34
stranger–father relations, 44–7, 114, 131
structural adjustment programmes, 23,
    106
subject formation, 29

tales of origin, 1–11
taxation, 100